The Academic Self

DONALD E. HALL

The Academic Self

An Owner's Manual

THE OHIO STATE UNIVERSITY PRESS
Columbus

Library of Congress Cataloguing-in-Publication Data
    Hall, Donald E. (Donald Eugene), 1960–
    The academic self : an owner's manual / Donald E. Hall.
    p. cm.
    Includes bibliographical references (p.).
    ISBN 0-8142-0907-6 (alk. paper)—ISBN 0-8142-5099-8 (pbk. : alk. paper)
    1. College teachers—Job satisfaction. 2. College teachers—Intellectual life.
    3. College teaching—Vocational guidance. 4. Learning and scholarship.
    I. Title.
    LB2331.H3122 2002
    378.1'12—dc21

                                        2002005459

Cover and text design by Jennifer Shoffey Carr
Type set in Adobe Granjon
Printed by Thomson-Shore

The paper used in this publication meets the mimimum requirement of the American National Standard for Information Sciences—Permanence of Paper for Printed
Library Materials. ANSI Z39.48-1992

9 8 7 6 5 4 3 2

S oon my own anger was explained and done with;
but curiosity remained.
How explain the anger of the professors?
Why were they angry?

—VIRGINIA WOOLF
A Room of One's Own (1929)

· · · · · · · · · ·

Contents

. . . .

Acknowledgments

t HIS BOOK WOULD have been impossible without the support and wisdom of all of my fine colleagues at California State University, Northridge. They continue to amaze me with their energy, determination, and commitment to students. And those students were also key to the production of this book. My concern for them and the quality of their education and institutional environment has led me to a greater degree of candor here than I might have projected when first thinking about this project. If I speak too bluntly for some readers and acquaintances, I apologize, but I do so because I am often deeply worried about our profession and the impact of our attitudes and behaviors on each other and our students.

I would like to recognize the vitality and important work of the administration of Cal State Northridge. If I have avoided the cynicism regarding administration that plagues many academics, it is perhaps because I have been affiliated with so many hardworking, honest, and concerned administrators at Northridge, including Presidents Blenda Wilson and Jolene Koester, Provost Louanne Kennedy, Dean Jorge Garcia, and the chair of the Department of English, Robert Noreen.

I would like to express my gratitude to the members of the English program of the University of the Incarnate Word in San Antonio, Texas, for sharing with me their responses to some of my published work on the profession. Professors Hector Perez, Patricia Lochnar-Fite,

Matthias Schubnell, Moumin Quazi, Rebecca Hettich, and Jo LeCoeur all helped me think through some of the concepts I discuss here. Similarly, the faculty and students of the University of Victoria, Canada, patiently listened and helpfully responded to some very rough presentations of key chapters of this book.

Some material scattered throughout *The Academic Self* was published first in very different forms in MLA's *Profession 1999* and *Profession 2000;* in the Association of Department of English's *ADE Bulletin* (Fall 2001); and in my introduction to *Professions: Conversations on the Future of Literary and Cultural Studies,* published by the University of Illinois Press (2001). To the extent that I draw on that material, it is reprinted by permission of the copyright owners, the Modern Language Association of America, the Association of Departments of English, and the University of Illinois Press. I thank those institutions for the right to rework and reprint that material here.

I also wish to express my sincere thanks to Ohio State University Press and its current and former staff: Heather Lee Miller, Malcolm Litchfield, and Darrin Pratt. Two outside readers for the press offered invaluable support and advice; one was anonymous, the other was Professor Elaine Showalter of Princeton University. I greatly appreciate their commentaries.

Finally, I would like to acknowledge two individuals without whom this book could not have been written. William Ko Maruyama is the most important person in my life. His patience and love, and gentle tolerance of my scheduling and work habits, make him my shining star.

R. Baird Shuman taught me many and enduring lessons about the skepticism and irreverence necessary for a happy life in the academy. I can never repay that debt. It is to Bob Shuman that I dedicate this book.

· · · · · · · · · ·

Owning Up to Academic Dysfunctions

i N 1999 I PUBLISHED a brief essay in the Modern Language Association's annual publication *Profession* that generated a surprising amount of attention. Entitled "Professional Life (and Death) Under a Four-Four Teaching Load," the piece offered some practical strategies for graduate students and new assistant professors when faced with career possibilities and institutional demands for which their graduate training had not well prepared them. From anecdotal accounts, I know that the essay was passed around and discussed informally by faculty at colleges and universities across the country; it even spawned a panel discussion of responses at the South Central Modern Language Association (SCMLA) Conference in November 2000, arranged by Hector Perez, the coordinator of the English Department at the University of the Incarnate Word. He opened the panel by mentioning that he "was so taken by the issues raised by Hall that [he] immediately ran copies of the article and placed them in [his] department colleagues' boxes" (1). Why such a response? Very few individuals employed at institutions not defined as "Research 1" had ever spoken out of their particular position and experience base regarding the job search and career management. And I certainly felt (and feel) that there was (and is) much more to say. After discussing various possibilities with an editor at Ohio State University Press, I decided to try my hand at a longer project, aimed at the same audience, and offering more extended commentary on career planning, goal setting, and time management. Indeed, after a few false starts and what I now recognize as useful free writing (that I thought at the time was final draft writing) what you have before you is that book.

But there were some false starts and delays that have certainly challenged me to put into practice many of the concepts, principles, and talking points that I offer to my readers in the coming pages. Over the past months I have had to revise my own project schedule and topic outline many times as I have rethought the component parts of this book. And beyond those inevitable process-related bumps and modifications (a topic that I discuss in chapter 3), I have also had to remind myself of something that I emphasize in chapter 4: namely, that what is in the past cannot be altered, that lingering grudges only hinder our work in the present if we fail to recognize and then let go of them. How does that pertain to the project at hand? As was the case, no doubt, with many readers of this book, I came out of graduate school into the world of academic employment (in the early 1990s) grateful for having found a job, but with a profound sense of shock concerning the limitations of my training when compared to the realities of the profession in which I suddenly found myself. Indeed, friends and colleagues gradually detected in me a simmering resentment over the skewed and unrealistic nature of my own graduate education, as well as its continuing norms, even though I was very much inside of those feelings and therefore poorly positioned to perceive them. As I will emphasize throughout this book, we must often rely upon each other to fill in such gaps. Thus when I was describing this project to a colleague (almost ten years after finishing my graduate work, of course), she said something very telling: "I'm glad you are writing that book; it will be very cathartic for you." That comment stunned me and made me step back and reevaluate thoroughly the tone and content of my work to that point. Personal catharsis was not what I was trying to achieve.

Yet if I did hold on to some anger and frustration after leaving graduate school so many years earlier, I don't want to ignore the reasons why, for my own frustrations are hardly unique and will allow me here to open up a discussion of professorial life and some of the behavioral and attitudinal consequences of graduate school training for those of us entering a career in the academy. Certainly we all have our own reasons for pursuing such a career in spite of the long years of master's- and doctoral-level studies, the arduous process of writing a dissertation, and the terrible uncertainties of the job market. But one common hope among those with whom I attended graduate school and whom I meet today at academic conferences was and remains the desire to live a professional life constituted on principles of energetic and forthright intellectual activity in which one's broad theoretical beliefs, passionate devotion to lively and creative thought, and eager tackling of the most difficult questions of interpretation and identity could be incorporated into one's daily work. As graduate students, many of my colleagues and I hoped to find ourselves in a professional environment in which the supple give and take and energetic exploration of new ideas that we often found in our late-night discussions over coffee or beer (and occasionally in our graduate seminars), would be fostered, perhaps even dramatically intensified. After all, the debilitating anxieties we experienced over writing a dissertation and finding a job would be alleviated, would they not?

Instead, what many of us found in our new jobs (if we were lucky enough to get one, of course) was stunningly different from anything we had imagined: cynical senior colleagues (many of whom were suspicious of junior faculty, and some of whom actively scornful of their new colleagues' ideas and perspectives); heavy teaching loads that our research university mentors had never encountered or even mentioned to us; mid-career or seasoned junior colleagues who were horribly stressed and well on their way to a state of "burnout"; and too often a tense, competitive atmosphere in which personal achievement (often the single-minded pursuit of "stardom") was valued over collegial exchange and communal responsibility. While we had certainly heard rumors of departmental tensions, had often seen a certain inexplicable joylessness in our mentors' work (which translated into some very dreary graduate seminars, indeed), and had been steadily acculturated into a set of competitive professional norms, the realities of daily life in the academy were stunning and disappointing: widespread defensiveness and closed-mindedness, an all-too-common resentment of the achievement of colleagues, and often a paralyzing anxiety concerning one's own level of achievement.

I will discuss at length in later chapters some of the reasons behind such destructive/dysfunctional behavior in the academy and why professors often are the way they are (or rather, behave the ways they behave), but I do want to mention an obvious, though rarely discussed, cause here. As much as our research and writing today in English departments and the humanities are generally devoted to "cultural studies," are driven by and focused on an exploration of hierarchized and often invisible sociocultural binaries, we have yet to engage critically or even discuss openly our own hierarchies and binaries, especially those underlying our conception of "success" in our professional lives. While we are very adept at discussing the texts of novels, plays, poems, film, advertising, and even television shows, we are usually very reticent, if not wholly unwilling, to examine the textuality of our own profession, its scripts, values, biases, and behavioral norms. To be sure, we in the academy *are* discussing "professionalism" with increasing frequency, but in doing so, we seem to focus solely on the mechanical aspects of vita building and credentialization without ever examining the ways we act and the values we enact as we engage in professionalization, or the ways in which we interact with colleagues as they too engage in a process of career planning and development. We never even seem to ask the simple question, "why are we doing what we are doing?" Instead we focus obsessively on how to do as others do, or more accurately, how to do *better* than they do.

I certainly have no quarrel with those who extol the benefits of professional studies and professionalization among graduate students. With a knowledge of the "hows" in the profession can come confidence and the ability to make informed decisions about one's own career and its intersection with one's personal life. Yet the "whys" of the profession and a life in the academy certainly need intense scrutiny as well, and even the "hows" need approaching in a very different fashion than how they are treated commonly today. A discussion of "how" to succeed in one's professional life is woefully incomplete if it doesn't engage critically the notion of "success" as it is defined narrowly at research universities, in their graduate programs, and often well beyond. Indeed, as much as "performativity" is a buzzword, even a cliché, in departments of English and cultural studies, those emerging from doctoral programs often do so with only one professional "script" at hand: that of their own research university professors.

But as relatively narrow as the discussion on the "profession" has been to date, I still hold out a tremendous amount of hope that we *can* thoroughly critique the values of our work lives, that we can challenge and change those norms, attitudes, and behaviors that are intellectually and ethically indefensible (even if often understandable because of group pressures and institutionally generated stresses). Whatever draws people to the academic profession or to graduate school in the humanities, at the very least those who thrive there are almost always very adept readers of texts. There is enormous untapped potential therein, though certainly the actual situation is often far worse than simply one of "untapped potential." As Cathy N. Davidson accurately notes in an essay appearing in MLA's *Profession 2000*, "Our profession's particular gift to the world—our critical, intense, trained, sometimes skeptical, but always skilled habit of attentive reading—is sometimes our curse to ourselves. The border between close, critical reading (of texts, of people) and simple paranoia is sometimes all too permeable" (102). *The Academic Self: An Owner's Manual* argues that there is a way out of the paradox that she isolates (that our gift to the world can be *our curse* to ourselves). After all, we *are* skillful readers, but we must own up to the fact that far too rarely are our own professional "selves" part of our close, and especially, our critical reading projects.

That is what *The Academic Self* sets out to do: encourage its readership to engage critically their professional self-identities, processes, values, and definitions of success. It asks its readers to confront head-on their own complicities with and/or critical stances toward the diagnosis offered by Deborah Tannen in her discussion of "Agonism in the Academy": "The way we train our students, conduct our classes and our research, and exchange ideas at meetings and in print are all driven by our ideological assumption that intellectual inquiry is a metaphorical battle. Following from that is a second assumption, that the best way to demonstrate intellectual prowess is to criticize, find fault, and attack" (B7). To what extent and how can we do the "self"-critical work needed to challenge such norms? This book's methodology draws broadly on sociologist Anthony Giddens's theories of self-identity and reflexivity, which I will discuss more fully in chapter 1. I ask my readers to "own" their self-identities, not in the sense of claiming or attempting to exercise absolute control over them but rather of *owning up to* their own behaviors, attitudes, and complicities with certain entrenched professional hierarchies, and also their responsibility for challenging and changing those that are finally unsupportable or indefensible. And in doing so, this book does not simply issue abstract calls for change. Rather, I try to couple any exhortations with clear, concrete, and practical strategies for responding productively (rather than destructively) to the many uncertainties of academic life.

While *The Academic Self* is written primarily for an audience of graduate students and junior faculty, it invites into its discussion academics at all stages in their work lives, at the same time that it recognizes how busy those lives often are. Designed as a quick read (we are all already overwhelmed by other necessary reading), it is actually set up as something of a brief "self"-study course (or course on the study of the self). Yet as succinctly as it may express itself, certainly what *The Academic Self* asks for is far from easy.

I pose here some difficult questions that most books on the academy have simply ignored. In focusing directly on uninterrogated professional norms and communal dynamics, and on our individual acts of complicity with them, *The Academic Self* differs fundamentally from its most closely allied predecessor, Emily Toth's Ms. *Mentor's Impeccable Advice for Women in Academia*. Toth's widely read book offers some pointed and useful advice on short-term self-protective strategies for women (and, actually, men, too) as they move through graduate school, the job search, and the tenure process. But then her discussion ends abruptly, stopping short of a call for any precise changes in our collective behavior or the fundamental attitudes that underlie many of the oppressive situations she so accurately describes:

> Midlife, Ms. Mentor declares, is a time to improve one's teaching and one's ability to communicate life's truths (and to find out what the truths are). It is your opportunity to mold young minds, to mentor them, to show them the pleasures of the intellect and the joys of gossip. Freed from the fear of tenure denial, buoyed by a gaggle of feisty feminist friends, a mid-life woman can be witty and clever and anecdotal, and even foul-mouthed if she'd like to be.
>
> She cannot be Ms. Mentor, of course, but she can be someone almost as wise and fine. She can be herself. (201)

Well, perhaps. But nowhere does Toth explore and critically engage the professional "mold" into which her readers should press (if that is the appropriate verb) aspiring academics, beyond that exemplified in the self-protective strategies she discusses. The "self" she mentions will hardly be "freed" overnight from its dependence on well-rehearsed maneuvers and entrenched, competitive behaviors; it has already been thoroughly professionalized as defensively poised.

Unlike Toth, I believe that life's "truths" need questioning in sustained fashion and long before midlife, or they may never be questioned at all, and that the professional self (whether herself or himself) needs carefully reflecting upon, too, or the base-level fearfulness and then facile resort to "gossipy" deployment of power over others (which are hardly aspects of academic women's selfhood alone) will be naturalized as continuing components of one's professorial identity. Frankly, even the liberation that Toth announces is not very appealing; I'm weary of academics (male and female) being as "wise" and "foul-mouthed" (and often foul-tempered) as they would "like to be," especially when bent on communicating "life's truths." And too many of us may already be a little too "clever" for our own good, trapped in a dynamic of pernicious anxiety over being "found out," discovered to be human and fallible rather than consistently fine, witty, and wise.

I am hardly fearless, but my fears are different. From my graduate school days to the present, I have been much more afraid of intellectual stupor and hypocrisy—especially that evinced and reinforced in the nervous avoidance of difficult issues of authority and identity—than I have been of risking embarrassment, a job, or a promotion. Maybe that willingness to risk is partially, even largely, because I am male, white, and (middle) class-privileged. I acknowledge fully that possibility, but what I have found most fearful of all is that so few academics, whatever their gender, ethnicity, sexuality, or class background, seem willing *ever* to challenge the behavioral norms of our profession, even after the supposed "freedom" of tenure. Far too often tenure simply means the freedom to be as unreflective as we would like to be.

That lack of critical self-examination is wholly inconsistent with what I and others believe is the specific and most pressing responsibility of the intellectual (especially, I might add, the tenured, job-protected, and therefore highly privileged intellectual). In a superb little book entitled *Foucault and Social Dialogue*, philosopher Christopher Falzon teases out an important line of thought running through much of Michel Foucault's work that has made Foucault by far the most important influence on my own thought and work, even when I disagree with some of his generalizations and conclusions. I will quote Falzon at length here because he so clearly pinpoints the challenge issued in Foucault's work that the present book amplifies vis-à-vis our own professorial self-identities:

[T]he problematisation of our prevailing forms of life in order to promote resistance and new forms of thinking and acting, is, for Foucault, central to the life of the philosopher, the thinker, the intellectual. He comes to define thinking itself as a process of reflective problematisation. It is what allows one to step back from a way of acting and reacting, to "present it to oneself as an object of thought and question it as to its meaning, its conditions, its goals." Thought, he says, is "freedom in relation to what one does, the motion by which one detaches oneself from it, establishes it as an object, and reflects on it as a problem." And it is this idea of self-detachment that is at the heart of Foucault's conception of the "ethics of the intellectual." The role of the intellectual is not to "tell others what to do." Rather, one should "make oneself permanently capable of detaching oneself from oneself." That is, the specific role of the intellectual is to question over and over again what is postulated as self-evident, to reinterrogate the obvious and assumed, to unsettle habits and ways of thinking, and to dissipate accepted familiarities. (70)

I would modify those assertions significantly to recognize that "freedom" is, of course, impossible and that we can never succeed at wholly detaching ourselves from ourselves or achieve anything like clarity in our perspective on ourselves. Yet certainly the impulse to question, reinterrogate, unsettle, and dissipate familiarities should drive our work as intellectuals, and we— *our selves*—should hold no privileged position vis-à-vis that critical engagement. That we cannot see our "selves" clearly means that we must energetically solicit the articulated perspectives of others who can add immeasurably to our partial views, even if those views will, in fact, never be complete. Thus in ways clearly indebted to Foucault, my work here seeks to foster a "form of reflection which opposes deadening, unthinking closure and domination, opens thought up to the other, assists those who resist, promotes the revitalizing creation of new forms of thought and action, and ultimately fosters continuing dialogue" (Falzon 71).

Wholly incompatible with the work of this book would be the articulation of any set of static formulas or simple prescriptions for what is or is not a "successful" career. Definitions of success depend upon some very personal and painstaking decisions, as I will emphasize throughout my discussion and in my postscript to this book. But certainly there are some common definitions of success that I *will* question consistently here because they appear to lack that component of reflection already mentioned. While offering concrete strategies for professional goal setting and achievement, this book will reject, even as it attempts to understand, what is commonly called "careerism" (and what is somewhat differently known as "workaholism") as a static solution to what should be a continuing problematization. *The Academic Self* offers its readers some of the tools necessary for developing a successful career on one's "own" terms, so to speak, while also insisting that one's individual efforts are always part of a larger context of communal responsibilities, collegial support, and institutional needs.

Indeed, one of the most common objections to the work of books such as this one—which falls broadly within the category of "self-help" books—is that they emphasize individual strategies and personal responsibility but ignore communal dynamics and institutional and political contexts that may be impinging or oppressive. Such an objection was the thrust of a cogent response to my aforementioned essay published a year later in MLA's *Profession 2000*. Lisa Botshon and Siobhan Senier's article "The 'How-to' and Its Hazards in a Moment of Institutional Change" perhaps sums up the skepticism of many in stating,

> [T]he genre of self-help is finally more destructive than instructive. Like articles in *Cosmopolitan* that instruct women how to maintain their careers, keep their husbands satisfied, spend quality time with their children, and still boast sparkling kitchens such pieces focus our attention on personal energy and dilemmas at the expense of the more important battles we need to fight. The rise of the academic advice article should serve to call us back to the larger issues plaguing our profession, galvanizing us not to don dark glasses and trench coats so we can publish four books by the time we come up for tenure but to struggle collectively for better working conditions and vibrant intellectual communities. (171)

Their response has allowed me to clarify further some of my own points. What Botshon and Senier construct is, I believe, an unnecessary and false dichotomy. Indeed, at the conclusion of her own skeptical examination of the "self-help" movement to date, Eva Moskowitz says, "We need a politics and a therapeutics that are not mutually exclusive. . . . We must be wary of vapid public therapies while remaining open to the possibilities of a therapeutic politics that enhances social life" (284). That is the bridge that I am trying to make here. A collective struggle for better working conditions and a more vibrant intellectual community *can be* the central, defining component of any academic's or group of academics' career plan. In fact, nowhere in the "genre of self-help" (at least as I have reviewed the popular and academic literature) is political action and collective goal setting dismissed or disallowed. But certainly the genre does emphasize personal responsibility even in such broadly cast efforts. Unless I (or you) as an individual shoulder some responsibility for articulating, organizing, and participating in goal setting; unless we as a group of like-minded, perhaps politically radical, individuals organize our time carefully and understand the processes through which institutional change is effected; unless we self-reflect and understand how we, also as individuals working together, must schedule and plan thoughtfully so we can reliably commit our perhaps very limited time to group processes and still meet our individual goals for tenure and promotion, *change will never occur.*

Institutions may be horribly oppressive, relatively benign, or (usually) somewhere between those extremes, but they certainly make for convenient targets. Academics love to critique institutions because there is a certain tangible textuality to them, with their documents, written rules, and administrative structures. Yet we are not so comfortable contemplating our own textuality, our own motivations, priorities, fears, and ambitions. Indeed, part of the "ongoing, vibrant, and indispensable intellectual conversation" (Botshon and Senier 168) in which we should all engage concerns our own potentials, successes, and failures, and to what extent those are influenced by external forces and to what extent by our own sometimes mistaken choices, priorities, and strategies. Of course, such strategies can be collectively defined and targeted to effect quite radical institutional change. But the action groups seeking to bring about that change are made up of individuals *who must find the time to work together and figure out how to do so responsibly and amicably* or their efforts will fail miserably. Collective success is always based on personal behaviors and decisions, and on effective planning. Too often we simply complain that "someone" should do "something" about a situation that we perceive, but we never seem to find the energy, the motivation, the collegial goodwill, or the hours in the day to do something about it ourselves.

This book is my attempt to "do something" about a set of problems I perceive. As indicated earlier, I am employed at what is known commonly as a "teaching school," one with a standard four-course-a-semester load. I feel incredibly lucky to have any job in this profession, but certainly I and my colleagues have had to strategize and prioritize carefully as we have met the demands of our institution for tenure and promotion, but also set and met our own goals for institutional change, program development, and research. At times our work has been collective in our efforts to create new curricula, alter the design of the English major, improve our department's communal/collegial dynamics, and fine-tune our hiring plans and priorities. At other times our work has been more solitary in the scholarship we have engaged in and the other solo projects we have initiated. But the happiest and most vibrant of us have learned well how to read the texts of our institution, our profession, our careers, and our own professorial self-identities, in open dialogue with each other, so that we have "succeeded" in multi-dimensional ways, even when the larger profession has looked at our institutional affiliation (which is far from prestigious) and implicitly or explicitly defined us otherwise.

It is from such a vantage point (as limited as it inevitably is) that I offer the perspectives and suggestions that follow. Some of the skills and strategies that I mention here are holdovers and refinements from my own graduate school days, but they are not ones I learned in seminars or professional studies workshops; rather they were those I acquired as I juggled writing a dissertation with teaching two classes and fulfilling the demands of a part-time library job that I kept to pay my bills. Indeed, one of the contributors to the SCMLA panel mentioned earlier spoke frankly about his own similar experience:

> Recently, I graduated from a Research Institution, the University of North Texas, whose professors taught under a 2-3 load. As a graduate student working on my Ph.D., usually taking two or three classes, I also taught as a teaching fellow (whose load was 2-2), and sometimes, near the end of my graduate career, was an adjunct at a local junior college, teaching two more courses. In a way, my actual load was five or six classes per semester, with the further expectation that I would prepare and pass my comps, submit a decent dissertation proposal, and complete my dissertation while doing a job search. In its own way, UNT prepared me well to teach, not in a research institution, but in a teaching school with a 4-4 load. My serious response to Donald Hall is that I don't know the difference yet. (Quazi, 1–2)

Indeed, many of us, perhaps the happiest of us, employed at "teaching schools" have found that as we move into our post-graduate school careers, we have not become "like" our graduate school professors; instead we have remained "like" we were in grad school: skeptical about the norms and values of the larger profession, self-protective when dealing with empowered faculty members, and very careful about time management and professional prioritization.

As is true for all academics, whatever their institutional affiliation, I have had to make very tough choices about what goals to set and how to use my time effectively in order to achieve them. My own institution's expectations for research have been modest, but I have set as a personal goal a continuing engagement with a broader context of scholarship and with the ongoing dialogue concerning our profession. I have found workable balances among teaching, service, and research so that my local and national careers have been "successful" as I have defined that term (but also with an understanding of the meaning-making contexts in which I have defined it). I have often had to revise my plans and even abandon projects that became impossible or too costly; such pragmatism is necessary if one wishes to remain an agent of change within the profession. But on the whole, I have had a very fulfilling career to date and offer here my reading of why and how that has been the case.

Each chapter of this book examines in succinct fashion a different component of one's professional self-identity. Chapter 1 examines the professorial "self" as a text, drawing on Anthony Giddens's theories of self-identity and reflexivity. Chapter 2 turns to the text of the larger academic profession, looking at its diversity and many component parts, and emphasizing the necessity of active career planning and goal setting with knowledge of that diversity. Chapter 3 examines the text of "process" and how to plan effectively in order to achieve well-thought-out short-, medium-, and long-term goals. Chapter 4 looks at the text of "collegiality" and how an individual working with groups of like-minded colleagues can contribute to and improve the dynamics of a department or institution. The postscript offers some personal reflections on how I have personally defined success and have found fulfillment in my work and beyond. Throughout this discussion, I use as a touchstone the concept of "ownership," reminding readers and myself that we must always recognize our own base-level responsibility for critically examining our goals, thoughtfully articulating them, and then carefully planning so that we can achieve them. As smart and verbally adept people, we academics are very good at shifting responsibility and talking our way out of any admissions of failure or complicity with dysfunctionality. Those are the very critical moves that seed the paranoia that Davidson identifies above.

~

Let me bring this introduction to a close by saying simply that as I sit here putting my final touches on it, I am forty-one years old and am fortunate to have made it to the rank of tenured, full professor a few years ago. I mention this not to self-congratulate, but because, as much as we might like to think of our work as "timeless," it is very much "in" and "of" time. Speaking out of actuarial probabilities I have another quarter of a century or so in my profession; what type of profession it is going to be is of profound interest to me. The issues that I raise here are real, they are not at all "academic" as some use that term: impractical or uselessly theoretical. What I hope I will find with increasing frequency is the suppleness, the humility, the eager, joyous engagement with new ideas, and the sense of multiple possibilities for and paths to success in this profession that I and many of my fellow graduate students had hoped we would find when we contemplated a career in the academy. I remain very optimistic in this regard. In one of the more useful chapters of a recent self-help bestseller—*Don't Sweat the Small Stuff at Work*—Richard Carlson urges his readers to "Light a Candle Instead of Cursing the Darkness." He writes,

> While we're working, it's easy to fall into the trap of spending our time and energy taking note and complaining about the wrongs of the world—the way things are, the economy, negative people, industry changes, greed, lack of compassion, bureaucracy, and so forth. After all, if we are looking for verification that the world is full of problems, we don't have to look far to prove our assumptions. . . .
>
> It's interesting, however, to notice that in many instances you cannot only make a dent in a problem, but actually reduce your own stress level in the process by simply choosing to "light a candle." Simply put, this means making a suggestion or taking a positive step toward improving a source of stress. It means putting increased emphasis on a potential solution and less emphasis on "cursing" the problem. (36–37)

He goes on to say that when you perceive a problem in your professional environment, "Gather together a few of your friends and gently bring the issue to the table." Suggest a solution and "Invite others to join you" (37) in working collectively toward that solution.

This book, you might say, is my candle and my invitation.

chapter one

. . . .

Self

i WANT TO RETURN for a moment to the observation that I
quoted in my introduction, drawn from Cathy Davidson's essay
"Them versus Us (and Which One of 'Them' Is Me?)": "Our profession's particular gift to the world—our critical, intense, trained, sometimes skeptical but always skilled habit of attentive reading—is
sometimes our curse to ourselves. The border between close, critical reading (of texts, of people) and simple paranoia is sometimes all too permeable" (102). Her response to the problems generated by this "skilled
habit of attentive reading"—in the form of several of the lessons that she
offers to her readers (ones that she has learned well during her years in
administration)—is to suggest that we all cultivate an openness to constructive criticism and that we also avoid hastiness in responding to the
rhetorical excesses and oppositional stances of others. I applaud her frank-
ness, and to say the least, wholeheartedly endorse these and her other
common-sense suggestions.

But I would like to think further about the particular paradox that
she isolates: namely, that our gift to the world can be our curse to ourselves. Why is it that our reading practices so often engender paranoia?
Indeed, in Davidson's words, "Why can't we get along?" (102) I could
spend a lot of time exploring certain methods of reading and certain theoretical stances that I believe too often inflame "us/them" thinking, but
that would be the subject of a different book. Instead, I suggest that to

1

begin to answer her timely question, we must consider a text that even Davidson ignores in her astute commentary: that of our own "selves," which also need to be part of our close, and especially, critical reading projects. This omission is sometimes one of explicit mention only, for many of us do self-reflect often, and certainly we engage in self-reflexive activity continuously. But that lack of explicit mention of why we must more regularly and skillfully engage in close, critical readings not only of print texts and of other people but also of our own attitudes and priorities is unfortunate and certainly abets some of the least defensible professional behaviors with which we are all well acquainted: professorial arrogance, hypocrisy, greediness, angry dismissal of others' arguments and even angrier envy of their accomplishments, and the many other traits that can contribute to the proverbial "snake-pit" atmosphere of some of our departments and universities.

In 1991, I was hired into a reputed "snake-pit"—a heavily factionalized department engaged in some very bitter internal struggles—but through a variety of transitions and other means (including early retirements, but even more importantly, some thoughtful planning discussions and careful hiring), concerned colleagues and I helped make it, a decade or so later, a fairly snake-free zone. I am hardly casting any of us as St. Patrick here, but simply as a group of concerned and committed individuals eagerly trying to make work—make functional rather than dysfunctional—our current and unalterable state of professional "dissensus," as described by Bill Readings in *The University in Ruins* and J. Hillis Miller in several recent works. Indeed, whenever I have served as hiring committee chair, I have opened interviews for all candidates seeking tenure-track positions within our department with the same prompt: "I would like to begin by offering you the opportunity to talk about your career plans and professional priorities. What goals are you setting for yourself as you embark on a career? Talk about the type of department or university setting that you imagine would be one in which you could thrive and meet those goals." The immediate response has often been, "Hmmm, good question." This buys the candidate a few seconds to engage in a quick assessment of his/her sense of professional self-identity, one which is then, no doubt, shaped somewhat and articulated to meet what is imagined as our expectations. Of course, such calculation will always play a part in the job-seeking process, and frankly, modest calculation and tailoring of responses do not concern me nearly as much as the potential wild inaccuracy of a candidate's response caused by its very hastiness. The answers elicited from the prompts above have been, for me, the most significant of the entire interview. In my experience, their length, thoughtfulness, and certainly content, can reveal accurately the degree of professional flexibility, potential for equanimity, and commitment to collegiality of the candidate in question. And these are the building blocks of a healthier and happier department.

But a few building blocks are not sufficient by themselves. Questions of goals and priorities are ones that all of us, not just job candidates, should be pondering throughout our careers. Furthermore, beyond simply believing that we should all be able to respond quickly and accurately to an inquiry concerning our sense of professional self-identity, I would even suggest that the qualities just mentioned—equanimity, collegiality, and flexibility—are themselves neither "naturally" occurring among some faculty nor innately present in some job candidates' personality types; they can be learned and developed through such self-aware self-reflexive activity.

Those who read current work in Anglo-European philosophy and sociology will probably recognize the term "reflexivity" immediately as one central to the theories of Anthony Giddens (and to a lesser extent, Ulrich Beck and others). In *The Consequences of Modernity*, *Modernity and Self-Identity*, and the collection *Reflexive Modernization*, Giddens offers extended commentary on the question of whether the present time constitutes a period of "post"-modernity or a continuation and intensification of certain key aspects of modernity itself. His position is the latter. What does strike him as unique about late twentieth- (and now twenty-first-) century Western life, however, is the unparalleled degree and social pervasiveness of what he terms "the reflexive construction of self-identity" (*Modernity and Self-Identity* 85), which I will shorten here to "self-reflexivity." As it applies to individuals, such self-reflexivity entails the seeing of one's life as a project always in the making, one that is not controlled by tradition or other external forces that may have played determining roles in the past (such as peer group norms or parental mandates). For Giddens, the late-modern "self is not a passive entity" at all (2); instead, "the self, like the broader institutional contexts in which it exists, has to be reflexively made" (3), and is thereby susceptible "to chronic revision in the light of new information or knowledge" (20). This personal agency-driven dynamic of continuing change is why Giddens and I use the terms "reflexivity" rather than "reflection" and "self-identity" rather than "identity":

> Since the self is a somewhat amorphous phenomenon, self-identity cannot refer merely to its persistence over time in the way philosophers might speak of the "identity" of objects or things. The "identity" of the self, in contrast to the self as a generic phenomenon, presumes reflexive awareness. It is what the individual is conscious "of" in the term "self-consciousness." Self-identity, in other words, is not something that is just given, as a result of the continuities of the individual's action-system, but something that has to be routinely created and sustained in the reflexive activities of the individual. (52)

Beyond examining the consequences of the many ways that traditional narratives of gender, sexuality, ethnicity, and class are eroding around us, Giddens explores how self-help books and competing—public, private, and professional—voices of authority on a wide variety of life issues allow and in many ways require the individual to make continuous choices that influence the course of his/her own existence. The result is a sense of potentially exhilarating freedom for the late-modern individual, but who is also always threatened by potentially debilitating anxiety about the consequences and sustainability of those choices.

Obviously, I am adding my own voice to that social conversation on the life choices we make, their consequences and sustainability, for it is my opinion that the always-threatening anxiety can only be assuaged by openly discussing, collectively exploring, and (yes, always imperfectly) recognizing both the limitations and potentials of our own agency. We intellectuals *certainly* have no credible excuse for anything like "self"-deception. Giddens notes accurately that one of the singular characteristics of our age is a "wholesale reflexivity—which of course includes reflection upon the nature of reflection itself" (*Consequences of Modernity* 39). This is, in fact, the basis of the optimism that motivates and pervades this book—that we academics are particularly well trained and able to reflect upon the nature of reflection and to act with a sharpened self-awareness therein and thereafter. Admittedly, intellectuals have been struggling with this potential since at least the time of Descartes. Even so, it is a "meta"-reflective move that I believe still has enormous transformative potential, if we recognize our own limitations and our need for the perspectives and commentary of others. Practically speaking, it is a form of agency that can start with a forthright admission of our own socially (or in this case, professionally) constructed selfhood. Many of the values, behaviors, and roles that are normalized in the academy, that are passed along as necessary components of professorhood, are in fact unnecessary and are *ab*-normalizable. One might think of this as the potential for "self-aware" self-reflexivity to differentiate it from forms of reflexivity that lack a sharp critical engagement and simply reproduce behaviors, hierarchies, and indefensible social/professional norms. Living in the late-modern age, in a social milieu already thoroughly pervaded by forms of self-reflexivity, and trained as skilled critical readers, we academics in particular have the capacity and the professional skills to live with a critical (self-) consciousness, *to reflect critically upon self-reflexivity*, and to use always our professional talents to integrate our theories and our practices. But this cannot be done in private, and it certainly cannot be done without allowing those "selves" to be critically engaged in open communal discussion.

Admittedly, it is no easy task. As critics and theorists, we rarely discuss self-consciousness even when we single out other forms of consciousness—social consciousness, political consciousness, and the like—as highly desirable in our work. This is hardly surprising, for self-consciousness can be a terrible state of social and professional incapacitation. In its most extreme manifestation—as an actual obsession with the self as a highly fragile construct, always threatened by the scrutiny and judgment of others—self-consciousness is clearly a problem requiring intense therapeutic or psychiatric attention. However, in its much more common, nonobsessive manifestations, self-consciousness is actually a necessary part of a process of professional re-definition and goal setting. In fact, we can return often to the professional self as "text" without risking paralysis if we first modify our expectations of a single legitimate definition of, and seamless and incontrovertibly authoritative performance of, the academic self.

The term *self-consciousness* means at least two different things: a private consciousness of our own selfhood—and specifically its constructed nature—and an awareness of our "selves" as objects of social scrutiny. Almost anyone in (or out of) our profession would agree that the latter evokes the most intense fear, namely, of being on display and being "found out." But this is the case, I would suggest, because our sense of being on display and "found out" returns us so continuously and unavoidably to the even more fundamentally, ontologically unsettling fact of our own "constructedness." And what makes this fact so unsettling? We academics are fully subject to broad social and paradigmatic changes, even as we act often as very adept commentators upon those changes. We can forget that fact as we "read" texts from a safe distance. Our base-level awareness of our "selves" as socially (and, to a varying degree, self-) created beings and as potentially fragile constructs is part and parcel of a general breakdown in the stable reliance upon transcendent meaning and fixed social definitions that characterized premodern eras. Indeed, our own concern with self-consciousness (and its potentially paralyzing effects) is only an intensification of well-documented nineteenth-century anxieties. In his 1831 essay "Characteristics," Thomas Carlyle declares "Self-contemplation" to be "infallibly the symptom of disease" (41). He goes on to say, "the sign of right performance is Unconsciousness" (45), which he equates with "pure unmixed life," while consciousness is a "diseased mixture and conflict of life and death" (48). Self-contemplation is thereby linked fundamentally—and I believe quite accurately—with the fact of *mortality*, a recognition of possible meaninglessness and an awareness of finitude.

Indeed, to be conscious of the self is always potentially to be paralyzed by a confrontation with one's own limitations: temporal, cognitive, and certainly metaphysical. For the intellectual (as for everyone), the always-threatening crisis is how to continue to *make meaning* in the midst of fundamental, existential meaninglessness. Carlyle's answer was one that will be familiar to many of my readers: a drowning out of fear and doubt through something like our contemporary notion of "workaholism." Others have reacted far, far differently. I think inevitably here of a fictional character, also from the Victorian era, whose presence continues to haunt our profession: Edward Casaubon from George Eliot's 1872 novel *Middlemarch*. Casaubon, the husband of the novel's heroine Dorothea, is a religious historian and textual critic who is writing (actually neurotically *not* writing) a book entitled *The Key to All Mythologies*. Eliot writes that "Mr. Casaubon . . . was the centre of his own world" (84), but that centrality certainly does not lead to anything like forthright self-reflexivity: "Mr. Casaubon had an intense consciousness within him and was spiritually a-hungered . . . [but] his soul was sensitive without being enthusiastic: it was too languid to thrill out of self-consciousness into passionate delight; it went on fluttering in the swampy ground where it was hatched, thinking of its wings and never flying" (272–73). Eliot muses, "The tenacity with which he strove to hide this inward drama made it the more vivid for him, as we hear with the more keenness what we wish others not to hear. Instead of wondering at this result of misery in Mr. Casaubon, I think it quite ordinary. Will not a tiny speck very close to our vision blot out the glory of the world and leave only a margin by which we see the blot? I know of no speck so troublesome as self" (407). Casaubon is self-conscious, self-absorbed, self-deceiving, and just plain selfish, without ever being self-aware in his self-reflexivity. He lives in the state of paranoia described by Davidson above. To be sure, Casaubon *is* self-reflexive, making choices continuously that impact his selfhood—among them, ignoring scholarship that renders passé his own research—and most of which actually compound his professional self-consciousness. But Casaubon never uses that self-consciousness as a spur to engage in a forthright remaking of his professional selfhood. Thus Casaubon lives in terror of exposure, anxious and anachronistic, dishonest with himself and others, miserable and misery-making.

Of course, Eliot has some sympathy for Casaubon, for as indicated above, his plight is not at all uncommon; she writes,

> For my part I am very sorry for him. It is an uneasy lot at best to be what we call highly taught and yet not to enjoy: to be present at this great spectacle of life and never to be liberated from a small, hungry, shivering self— never to be fully possessed by the glory we behold, never to have our consciousness rapturously transformed into the vividness of a thought, the ardour of a passion, the energy of an action, but always to be scholarly and uninspired, ambitious and timid, scrupulous and dimsighted. (273–74).

These words should press all of us into more forthright attention to our own self-reflexive responsibilities. While I, and no doubt many of my readers, would certainly question the possibility of ever being fully "liberated" from selfhood, perhaps we can agree on the need to use more effectively our already present liberation from notions of *fixed*, naturally occurring selfhood. This is certainly not as simple as Toth's liberation from the "fear of tenure" mentioned in my introduction, and it must be far more deliberate than Eliot's evocation of "rapture" would indicate. Casaubon's timidity and languor, his self-willed ignorance of competing theories, and his nervous avoidance of information that would challenge his own primacy all lead to a wholesale inability to reap the benefits of self-reflexivity at the same time that the anxieties that come from the new social fluidity and breakdown of insularity and tradition represented by his young cousin Will Ladislaw simply cannot be avoided. Casaubon exemplifies the modern scholar suffering all of the traumas of the dawning of reflexive modernization and none of the benefits.

But if, in Carlyle's words, self-consciousness is a disease (at least potentially, anyway) sapping our energy and ability to live happily and productively, his own stated cure certainly should give us pause: "man is actually Here; not to ask questions, but to do work" (57). Carlyle concludes, "Here on Earth we are Soldiers, fighting in a foreign land; that understand not the plan of the campaign, and have no need to understand it; seeing well what is at our hand to be done. Let us do it like Soldiers; with submission, with courage, with a heroic joy. 'Whatsoever thy hand findeth to do, do it with all thy might'" (69). Indeed, this possibility of hyperactively "working" oneself out of self-consciousness remains a very seductive one. We all know that work relentlessly performed can as effectively (and temporarily) numb the mind as alcohol or drugs. In the words of Al Gini (from his intriguing study *My Job, My Self*) work often becomes "a narcotic [that] insulates and isolates us" (122). Certainly, and as just indicated, "understanding" or anything approaching *critical* attachment has no role in Carlyle's prescription. Indeed, as we see with many of Carlyle's more infamous statements revealing his rank racism and classism, this numbing of consciousness means that the social implications of the work performed—and the way it is performed—will always remain largely unreflected upon. While relentlessly working one's way out of the paralysis of self-consciousness may feel like an answer to our worst fears, in choosing that option, we leave wholly undiscussed what I believe is our base-level responsibility for the making of intellectually and communally defensible meaning in our lives. After witnessing the consequences of some of the more horrific belief systems of the twentieth century, we should know well that any call for "work" that can make one "free" needs continuing and thorough interrogation.

These are the two extremes that continue to plague academic existence: that of Casaubonic paralysis and Carlylean workaholism. Neither is self-aware or honest, neither integrates our intellectual and theoretical beliefs with our practices in any defensible way; neither is communally responsive and responsible; and neither leads to anything like equanimity in our professional, or indeed personal, lives. In sum, both are avoidance strategies and make for both miserable and—in the communities of our departments, classrooms, and larger profession—misery-making existences.

This is where the concept of "ownership" pertains. If we are going to avoid the extremes just mentioned and work toward a professional existence that is intellectually vibrant; one that is responsive to our own needs and desires but also to our context, to our communal and institutional responsibilities, that recognizes our agency when and where it exists, but also the real limitations on that agency, then we must make a series of difficult, fundamental decisions. Do we recognize and embrace the fact that we choose our professional values, behaviors, and definitions of success in response to and negotiation with those provided by the professional community in which we exist? Furthermore, do we accept or attempt to deny the fact that we have chosen a profession in which we are on display in a myriad of ways? Certainly it is an odd profession of extremes that we have chosen. Some of our work is done in very solitary fashion—at our computers as we write or in quiet reading or paper-grading sessions—but at the other extreme much of it is done is very public fashion: in the teaching we do; in the department and committee work we perform; in the many ways our writing is read and commented upon by critics and other readers; and in the ways our work is judged for tenure, promotion, and even pay raise processes. In all these ways we are, in fact, *texts* on display for others to read and respond to, and that is a fact that we can either nervously avoid *or* admit, embrace, and work *with* rather than against. Indeed, if our professional norms, behaviors, and values comprise scripts of sorts—as those of us influenced by theories of performativity should readily admit—let us at least allow that they are scripts that can be more critically engaged than they are at present.

This meta-reflective move certainly undermines our sense of our own uniqueness, and even more so, our sense of professional autonomy and mastery. Of course none of us actually is wholly unique, autonomous, or masterful—we were socially and professionally normed, we exist in the communities of our departments, our classrooms, our readerships, our professional organizations, etc., and we are all partial and prone to error. It is my point here that we can either embrace the ways that we exist always in dialogue and constitutive relationships with others or we can choose anxiety by thinking of ourselves as masterful scholars and isolated intellectual beings. Both the Casaubonic and Carlylean extremes meet in their lack of self-reflection and lack of engagement with a community of critical dialogue. Both exist inevitably within that community but seek to ignore or drown out the voices surrounding the self.

Thus to return to the prompt that I offered to all potential new colleagues, an emphasis on "owning" one's professional self-identity entails a willingness to articulate one's values and priorities, a willingness to engage critically and openly one's sense of what a professor "is" and "does," a recognition of one's own agency in choosing one's values but also a consciousness of the ways in which those values are made and judged communally. This "ownership" of one's self-identity means a movement between and an awareness of the text of one's selfhood and the context in which that selfhood exists, a movement between and an awareness of personal agency and an acceptance of where and how agency is limited. It is to address overtly the constructed nature of professional selfhood, as well as our individual and collective ability to embrace, change, or reject aspects of that construction. It is to use our knowledge of and ability to work with the texts of theory and criticism in responding to our own professional textuality. It is to recognize that we do make meaning through our work and professional existence, and that the best we can do is to make intellectually, ethically, and communally defensible meaning. For only in openly discussing and defending that meaning (or those meanings) can we move from solipsism to self-aware self-reflexivity. Otherwise we will always be trapped inside of our own biases and self-serving beliefs.

～

As I admitted earlier, none of this is easy. In fact, it may be the hardest work we have to do, but also some of the most important. I am stating the obvious when I say that in any career, just as in any life, great challenges and changes will come. But while this observation may appear platitudinous, one question that it engenders is certainly worth considering at length: is it possible to teach, to foster, or even to learn an ability to respond to such uncertainties with flexibility and relative equanimity? While there is no guarantee of success, I believe that we can foreground certain aspects of our late-modern professional lives that will aid new (and seasoned) professionals in seeing their careers as ones always "in the making," never fixed to (or through) a single, simple set of goals, never fully within their control but certainly responsive to their self-reflexive activity, and never tied to a static, imposed narrative of "success" (and "failure") against which they have to judge always their accomplishments, circumstances, and choices.

Among the many possible starting points for such self-reflexive activity, I offer the following observations and provocations:

1. There is no one career path that guarantees success nor one set of accomplishments that signifies success.

Certainly this is an issue that we in the profession and those whom we train should grapple with much more honestly than we have to date. As many recent commentators have pointed out, any definition of professional success that depends upon the securing of a job at a research institution just like those at which we were all trained is also one through which almost all of us will be defined as "failures." On the other hand, we have the ability, both individually and micro-communally, to define professional success to reflect our own abilities and needs, and in response to the opportunities afforded us. We can always exercise some agency over how we will process the hierarchies of value that exist in our professional lives. Rankings of institutions, of types of scholarly work, of publication venues, and of balances among teaching, research, and service, exist as conventions in our profession, ones that are not meaningless (for certainly they can affect us materially) but that are also open to questioning and individual decision making regarding their personal weight and validity. As long as we educate ourselves concerning the professional consequences—wide-ranging and more local—of our individual decisions and are willing to accept those consequences (which I will argue is always a key aspect of "ownership"), we should feel fully empowered to revise personally larger constructs and hierarchies of value that may strike us as hollow or passé.

But if we decide to accept without substantial revision certain existing professional norms and values, it is also important to remember that "stellar" achievements can also bring enormous anxieties concerning one's ability to build on those achievements. We all know this is true concerning music, film, and fiction-writing careers, but we do not always admit its truth concerning academic careers. Unless we find ways of taking our successes as well as our failures as less than fully accurate indicators of the sum total of our fundamental worth in this world, we will be forever driven by a fear of failure rather than a love of learning or a commitment to students. Careerism in its anxious and voracious need for continuing, quantifiable achievement—a certain number of books or articles published, a certain hierarchical ranking of affiliated institutions and presses, a certain salary increase—is never satisfied or satisfiable. Self-aware professional self-reflexivity can allow us to identify and gain a perspective on the destructive forces at work in our drives for "success" as it is sometimes narrowly defined. This does not mean that we should not set and strive to achieve our goals in publication, teaching, and institutional policy making. But we can do so with a broader perspective that allows those goals to change when necessary and that sees such goals as constructs to which we attribute power and over which we can exercise some agency.

2. All our careers are also subject to certain forces beyond our control.

We spend a great deal of time in our professional lives, and in our discussions of those lives with graduate students and young colleagues, commenting on and fine-tuning the intricacies of the merit aspect of our careers. We judge students in class and in thesis/dissertation writing processes, and we judge each other in manuscript and grant reviews, and in hiring, tenure, and promotion processes. Our systems of evaluation often provide quasi-objective criteria (or certainly deemphasize subjective factors) in the procedures by which professional rewards are garnered: high grades, article and book publication, recognition for scholarship and teaching, and similar "vita" items that commonly signify success in our careers. Of course, none of us—certainly not I—would have it any other way. Consistency and well-thought-out (and well-explained) criteria are vital to the fairness and accuracy of our decisions and professional processes.

But what often gets lost in discussions of such professional credentialization is any recognition of the chance and nonformulaic aspects of our professional lives, successes, and failures. As I mention above, we like, perhaps desperately need, to believe that our successes are "real" and accurate signifiers of our considerable talent and worth. But there is a pernicious consequence to such an equation, for we can also process failure to receive specific rewards—the job we want, the article placement we desire—as objectively, accurately determined "failure" in our careers and/or lives. In a powerful section on "Ontological Security and Existential Anxiety" in *Modernity and Self-Identity*, Giddens discusses the pervasiveness of "shame" in our late-modern lives, which "bears directly on self-identity because it is essentially anxiety about the adequacy of the narrative by means of which the individual sustains a coherent biography" (65). "Shame depends on feelings of personal insufficiency" and "anxieties about inadequacies of self" (65). Yet I suggest that by broadening our discussion of how our professional "selves" are continuously judged and inevitably, at various times, found lacking, we might be able to assuage some of the anxieties, and particularly the shame, that can eat at our sense—and our students' nascent sense—of professional equanimity.

What can it hurt (except our ego, of course) for us to reveal to students and young colleagues that we seasoned and experienced academics fail at times in processes by which we are judged? Certainly no mentor ever revealed that fact to me. I thought all successful professors succeeded always, and that when I failed, it was "real" and potentially definitive in a way that I now know simply is not the case. Since then I have discovered that even highly "successful" professors' articles are sometimes turned down, their conference proposals are sometimes rejected, and their job applications are sometimes denied. Furthermore, even their striking "successes"—which they may fully merit—are, in fact, very chancy.

To help make my point here about demystifying our professional selfhoods, let me offer a personal anecdote, one that I have written about before (in the introduction to my recent collection *Professions*), but that I believe bears repeating. One day in mid-1989, when I was a doctoral student at the University of Maryland, I took a break from dissertation writing to go to a movie at a suburban shopping mall. I was a little early for the film, so I stopped at a used bookstore on the way to the mall to look around and kill time. Digging around aimlessly in a section of old hardbacks I came upon a little red book called *Victorian Tales for Girls*. It cost $4. I only had about $10 with me, but finally decided to forego a soda at the theater and bought the book. A few weeks later, I happened upon a posted announcement for the Victorians Institute Conference of 1990 that asked for papers on Victorian imperialism. No primary text that I was well acquainted with seemed appropriate, so I dug out that little red book and found in it a story by the British children's writer Juliana Horatia Ewing that sparked some ideas. The conference wanted unusually long papers; mine ran about fifteen pages. My paper was accepted and later well received. A few weeks after the conference and while on a search for some now-forgotten piece of information, I noticed, by chance, a call for articles for a special issue of the *Children's Literature Association Quarterly* on imperialism. They wanted essays of about fifteen to twenty pages, with the submission deadline just two weeks away. I hesitated momentarily but sent in the conference paper essentially unrevised. It was accepted. In the fall of 1990, when I was applying for jobs, I constructed a version of my application letter that marketed myself as a "children's literature specialist" on the basis, primarily, of that one essay (as well as a chapter of my dissertation on *Tom Brown's Schooldays* and a solid, though wholly self-acquired, base of knowledge in the field). I got over a dozen interviews that year, but only one in "children's literature," at Cal State Northridge. As time wore on, every job for which I interviewed went to another candidate; even CSUN offered its position first to someone else who eventually turned it down. It was late spring before I heard that I had a firm offer from CSUN. At that point, I had decided that without a job offer that year, I would pursue a degree and career in library science. And in any case, the following year the number of advertised jobs in English declined precipitously.

The reason I occasionally tell the story above to graduate students and repeat it here is simple. I am where I am today—a full professor with a relatively successful and certainly enjoyable career—because I had an extra fifteen minutes to kill before a movie and decided to buy a little red book instead of a Diet Coke. No *Victorian Tales for Girls*, no full professorship today. Now, of course (and I can hear some of my mentors' voices, because they have heard and responded to this narrative before) I have worked very hard, and wouldn't be where I am if I hadn't written publishable research, etc, etc. I'm not saying that merit has nothing to do with professional advancement. But the "merit" aspects of our work are overdiscussed and certainly overreliedupon, while we almost never talk about how our careers, practices, positions, and successes are very unpredictable. I believe it would be of considerable benefit to our profession if all employed, successful academics traced back a series of arbitrary occurrences that account for where they are and the successes that they have had. It might foster a humility that would allow us to speak to one another without the rigidity and implicit belief in our own "mastery" that seems to account for at least some our rancorous behavior. Certainly it would allow us to put any career failures in perspective as ones also affected by chance. Finally it might mean that we could speak to graduate students in ways that acknowledge their difficulties and that also assure them that if they do not end up in the careers that they (sometimes desperately) want that it is *not necessarily their fault*. Not a single one of us, in or out of this profession, has finally and definitively mastered anything. We are all fallible and rather frail no matter how long our vitae, how thick and ivy-covered the stone walls that buttress our offices and classrooms, or how enviable and mighty our positions of professional privilege.

This recognition, frequent reiteration, and even wide publication of evidence of our human fallibility and the highly contingent nature of our successes and failures can be a starting point, I believe, for self-aware professional self-reflexivity. It deflates our arrogance and undermines our fictions of seamless, professorial sufficiency. It helps us begin to sort out what we are, and are not, able to influence and exercise choice and limited forms of control over. It also allows a certain degree of equanimity as we engage in career building and take our chances in doing work that can be highly frustrating and that can meet with unpredictable results. And, just perhaps, it can allow us to remain flexible in our career goals and in our responses to changing conditions and new opportunities.

3. Even with the uncertainties of our work, we are able to decide how we will process and respond to the forces of chance and the hierarchies of value in our professional lives.

One of the aspects of self-reflexivity that Giddens discusses is the now widespread use of self-help books and other guides to careers, parenting skills, and the choices that individuals must make when faced with a myriad of possible paths, actions, and identity positions. Certainly I know many academics who secretly, or not so secretly, read self-help books as they deal with the various turmoils of career and personal life. I have no problem acknowledging that I keep a self-help book, or a similarly useful work in Eastern or Western philosophy, as part of my daily reading. Some of the most useful "help" that I have found in them concerning career issues has come from the field of cognitive psychology, in popular best-sellers such as David D. Burns's *Feeling Good* and Richard Carlson's *Don't Sweat the Small Stuff*. Such works emphasize our own agency in the way that we process and receive information or meet life/career challenges that have the potential power to unsettle us thoroughly. Every experienced academic reading this book knows how agitating and even derailing unhappy professional news and interactions can be. A rejection notice, a bad review, a disappointing teaching or departmental evaluation, a sneering comment from a colleague—any of these can cut us to the core of our professional selves.

Yet it is also important to recognize that our reactions to the incidents above can be destructive and career undermining far beyond the content or implications of the incident itself. I have seen colleagues enraged by even mildly critical reviews and who destroy relationships with colleagues and students after receiving even constructive criticism. Many of us have seen rejection notices and anxieties over not meeting expectations devastate colleagues, some of whom will never publish the books that they write or dream of writing and who, in the most extreme cases, lose promotions, positions, and even entire careers because they are trapped in anxiety and unable to process productively the inevitable turmoils of professional life. Shame, fear, and anger can paralyze us. But that does not have to be the case. As part of a discussion of professional self-reflexivity, we can emphasize and reflect on the control that we do have—not definitive forms of control over our careers or the events that make them up, but rather over how we will respond to the events and information that we encounter. While I am not suggesting (at least at this moment) that we assign self-help books such as those listed above in our graduate classes or for general departmental reading, certainly I am suggesting that we can articulate, emphasize, and remember that our lives and careers can be enhanced by—and often even depend upon—our flexibility and equanimity when confronted with difficulties. This is a form of self-awareness that, certainly, I have always looked for in interviews and other interactions with potential colleagues and professional collaborators. Where those qualities come from—whether from therapy, self-help books, or discussions with friends, colleagues, or family—is far less important than a recognition of their absolute necessity.

4. Our interests, goals, methodologies, and senses of professional self-identity may change dramatically over time.

Flexibility and suppleness are key to contentment in our professional lives, which is not to say that wishy-washy or unreliable behavior is ever commendable. Indeed, if we continue to reflect upon our communal lives and responsibilities and the ways that our actions impact others dramatically, our sense of responsibility will actually be heightened. Yet clearly we can broadly self-define as intellectuals, teachers, and colleagues in such a way that our interests and focuses can change in response not only to local needs but also to new information and interests, and surprising new possibilities.

If we are to incorporate this principle fully into our senses of professional self-identity, it must be met with institutional arrangements that allow for such mutability. If departments or universities define us narrowly and rigidly, we are clearly hampered in our own growth and ability to change. To be sure, an English department may, for good or not-so-good reasons, need a Milton course taught every semester, and I may be the only person hired for and qualified to teach such a course. I understand that my department may expect me to teach that course, even if my interests move elsewhere. A supple and collegial sense of professional self-identity and responsibility on my part would meet the needs of the department even as I make clear the necessity of finding another colleague to teach the course in the future (perhaps through hiring or through active inquiries of changing interests among current colleagues). A supple and collegial department administration would foster the growth of the individual department member and would respond to the demand just stated. To do otherwise would be to contribute administratively to burnout, bad teaching, waning scholarly productivity, and intellectual calcification among faculty.

5. In reflecting upon the constructed nature of our professional self-identities, we can remind ourselves always to work more honestly and forthrightly to integrate our theories and our practices.

I know this talking point will sound platitudinous to some, that "integrating theory and practice" is a cliché in our work today. But the reason it continues to be invoked, even if in clichéd fashion, is that it is so very rarely done. The disconnect between our complex and perception-altering theories and our starkly simplistic professional attitudes and actions can be stunning. Some graduate students reading this book will probably know immediately to what and whom I am referring here: "Marxist" professors who treat grad students like inmates in a workhouse; "feminist" professors who deploy power as harshly as any Roman dictator; "queer" professors who use their own work as a touchstone for new, rigidly enforced definitions of the "norm." I am fully sympathetic with all those theoretical stances; I simply hope to see them better integrated into our professional practices.

Beyond such stark cases of hypocrisy, there is a more serious problem in that the very nature of our work is often defined in base-level ways that need considerable intellectual complication. In *The Argument Culture* Deborah Tannen has a compelling section that speaks of "graduate school as boot camp," in which we are trained in "rigorous thinking, defined as the ability to launch and field verbal attacks" (266). Neither she nor I believe that rigorous thinking is anything other than the *sine qua non* of our professional and scholarly lives, but certainly some of the ways we define and manifest it can be highly problematic. Even as we teach binary-undermining theories and revisionary practices—of poststructuralism, postcoloniality, semiotics—we too often engage in professional behavior that evinces startling forms of "us/them" thinking. The binaries that continue to infect our professional lives are many, pernicious, and thoroughly "naturalized." For example, I remember a very famous and intellectually gifted scholar—well trained in contemporary theory—who once told me that she had only disdain for administrators, because "they are the enemy." Well, I am an administrator, and I am not her "enemy." The poststructuralist theories that she used in her critical writing and that she taught to students had done little to dislodge her own binary thinking in her professional life. Indeed, many of us continue to regard alternate theories and methodologies as "competing" with ours, or worse yet, competing with *us*. Our curricular and planning discussions often deteriorate into sparring sessions in which gray areas get lost and subtleties are reduced to ultimatums. As self-aware professionals we should be able to see alternate readings and alternative solutions to pressing problems as something other than hostile challenges to our core, fixed sense of self. "Us/them" thinking does not do justice to the complexity of our professional lives or our own intellectual training and capacities.

~

In my introduction, I promised an emphasis on the "practical" here, and that in spirit I would like to suggest a concrete way of normalizing more self-aware forms of self-reflexivity and make it a more regular, even common, subject of professional discussion. I believe that a brief statement of professional self-identity (the "professional statement," or "PS" for short here) might be as widely expected a part of our professional self-presentation as the curriculum vita currently is. Indeed, we expect a succinct but thoughtful "personal statement" as an important component of applications for graduate programs; a more mature version of it might also be part of all job searches, all applications for appointments or grants, and all occasions in which we professionally self-present (such as introducing ourselves in writing to colleagues, editors, etc.); it might even serve as the central texts of professional studies workshops and roundtables. Indeed, we can choose to make the texts of our own professional self-identities as important, as densely, eagerly interpreted as any other set of texts with which we commonly engage. By no means am I calling for wholesale self-absorption; texts of professional self-identity will hardly replace those of literature, film, and the visual arts as our primary objects of critical scrutiny. But I am suggesting that we move forthrightly from nervous avoidance to overt discussion of our identities as professional texts. That we do not do such critical work *at all* now is much more disturbing than the fact that we may occasionally appear self-absorbed if we do engage openly and critically with our professional selves.

Even beyond their utility in larger professional processes and venues, professional statements can also serve a more private and perhaps far more important purpose. Any such statement of professional self-identity should be used as a personal touchstone; it is one's statement to oneself about a career in the making—an individual mission statement, of sorts—that serves as a centering device, even as new opportunities arise that need careful evaluation. As a living and changing document, it provides the drawing board upon which one conceptualizes and reconceptualizes a professional life. It prods one to *remember* when convenient (and often destructive) forgetting or inconvenient (and often very destructive) distraction can serve all too easily to derail one's sense of purpose and energetic attachment to projects and long-term priorities. While it should never be rigid or mechanical, a professional statement should be considered an explicit contract with oneself that should be taken seriously, even as it is inevitably revisited and revised as one's life and priorities change. Indeed, the fact that I am asking that it also be made "public" reflects my belief that our careers and their components should be conceptualized always as parts of communal processes, prioritizations, and planning.

What might such a statement of professional self-identity entail? It would be a statement of ownership, one of self-aware responsibility taking and decision making. Certainly it should be succinct, however long and discursive a process it may take to arrive at it. A PS might run no longer than a standard dissertation abstract and would cover its points concisely and precisely, perhaps in 500 or so words (and in standardizing the circulation of such statements, we might dispense with the long application letters that are common in our profession; those cover letters could then speak more quickly and directly to the issue at hand). At a minimum, a PS—whether for one's own or others' use—would detail one's professional priorities and values and would articulate key goals. Depending upon one's self-conception, it might describe one's methodological or theoretical orientation or set of influences, one's pedagogy, and/or one's priorities concerning service, administrative, or programmatic work. It might engage explicitly or implicitly some of the broad "talking points" concerning our professional selves that I offered above and that I will explore in later chapters.

Obviously, there are topics that should be avoided in any publicly circulated professional statement. There is no reason to reveal information that could be used against one or personal data that is irrelevant to a particular process (marital status, race, physical disability, sexuality) unless one decides that such information is so integral to one's professional self-identity that disclosure is vital. Similarly it is a personal decision about the degree to which and how one talks about one's professional self-identity as firmly fixed or as supple and open to change. Certainly I have always wanted to hear about what job applicants, especially, have learned and how they have changed in the past in response to challenging situations—pedagogical or professional—but others might read such flexibility as inconsistency and changes as damning failures in previous strategies. This is a gray area where individuals should decide what aspects of the history of their professional self-identities are truly accurate indicators of their current states and future paths.

But I so firmly believe that an honest and widespread publication of frank statements of professional self-identity is key to changing the very nature of our discussion about our profession, that, putting my own words into action, my own draft professional statement is included as an appendix to this book. Whether or not we move as a profession toward the circulation of such statements, my PS is what I have used and will continue to use in my own processes of career planning and decision making. By the time this book is actually in print, it will have changed, no doubt, in some of its specifics, but its core values and broadest expressions will certainly endure. Of course, neither it nor any of the talking points discussed here or in later chapters is meant as prescriptive for anyone else's careers or decisions about priorities, only as starting points for an ongoing discussion that challenges the norms of closed, defensive professional self-identity, and perhaps, the paranoia it fosters.

Finally, it is important to remember that such overt professional self-reflexivity is not a panacea nor is its perfectly self-aware enactment ever possible: we cannot know ourselves fully, which is why I believe that continued dialogue is an essential component of it. But what is possible, I believe, is to self-reflect, self-construct, and self-reconstruct in ways that make our personal interactions and professional processes far less disabling. This remains one of the great potentials inherent in "professional studies," for in studying not only our profession but also our many possible professional selves, we can come to a fuller appreciation of our colleagues, students, and our administrators. Furthermore, we may be much better able to exercise agency in a larger sociopolitical context in which others are self-aware in their own self-reflexive activity and are often able to act with the complex vision and strategic suppleness acquired thereby.

chapter two

· · · · · · · · · · · · ·

Profession

i F INDIVIDUALS IN the academy have self-identities, the core values and belief structures of which should never be considered "natural" or self-evident, so too are the institutional contexts and cultures of our profession characterized by a diversity that is dramatic and in need of disclosure as well as sustained critical scrutiny. The *fact* of such diversity should not distress us at all (though some oppressive situations definitely should); rather, it is our response—actually, our all-too-common lack of response—to diversity that is often troubling. While chairing numerous hiring committees, interviewing dozens of candidates, and witnessing the shock that crossed countless faces when I discussed the four-course-per-semester teaching assignment at my university (and throughout most of the California State University system), I was struck by the fact that far too little discussion occurs within graduate programs and our professional organizations about life at any type of institution other than research universities. The general silence and uninterrogated misconceptions about life at teaching schools (here defined as those with a three-three assignment or higher) is hardly surprising; after all, few faculty mentoring graduate students and leading professional studies seminars have ever taught a heavy teaching assignment, and almost all books on our profession have been written by faculty at the same Ph.D.-granting institutions who have, undeniably, more time to devote to writing book-length works.

Yet, at the same time, a recent report by the MLA's Committee on Professional Employment notes that "the vast majority of Ph.D. students today will have careers that do not replicate those of their graduate school professors" and recommends accordingly that more information be provided to graduates about the "full range of job opportunities" within the "complex system of postsecondary and secondary education in this country" (32). In a 1995 *ADFL Bulletin* article, Herbert Lindenberger urges graduate professors to find ways of better informing students about "what would be expected of them in the various positions—whether in small liberal arts colleges, in big state schools without Ph.D. programs, or in community colleges—that they might one day be invited to fill" (8). I agree wholeheartedly but would add that such information must be discussed *more carefully* as well as *more often,* and certainly without any implicit biases that can relegate work at teaching institutions to categories of marginality, mediocrity, or professional "failure."

Indeed, the lack of well-informed discussions about professional life outside of the small number of research schools is unfortunate for several reasons. Certainly those hard-working academics employed at schools that emphasize teaching rather than research often feel misunderstood, undervalued, or ignored by the profession as a whole. But even more important is the fact that the new assistant professors whom they hire are often ill-equipped to deal with the pressures, as well as the potentials, of their new jobs. The fears they often express are ones that can, in fact, come to pass, especially if perceived and accepted as foregone conclusions. Once employed at teaching schools, young academics may indeed break productive connections with the larger profession; fall out of the conversation in their fields of specialization; and sink into silence and resentment under the weight of papers, exams, and committee work.

But such a fate is not a foregone conclusion. Clearly our profession must do a better job at welcoming voices and perspectives from across its diverse landscape in order to better train new academics and more fully appreciate the varieties of work that are performed. But those of us currently or formerly employed at institutions outside of the small number of research universities also have responsibilities and decisions. We must speak out about the pressures and potentials inherent in such work, and at the same time, acknowledge our own responsibility for constructing a career that satisfies us. A multifaceted, nationally resonant, and engaged professional life is quite possible while one is employed at a school whose primary mission is teaching, if that is the type of life that one commits oneself to pursuing. A life largely devoted to teaching is also quite possible. But however we might define our professional priorities, unless we speak honestly and often about the range of lives and careers across the landscape of our profession and our ways of finding fulfillment in them, we will continue to perpetuate the very debilitating myth that only those very few students who land jobs at research institutions are successes, that the rest (the great majority) have failed already or will fail inevitably in their pursuit of a vital professional life that includes, in whatever necessary or chosen balance, scholarship, teaching, and service.

Thus I want to expand on Bill Readings's discussion in *The University in Ruins* of the "dissensus" of our profession, by which he means that today there are no "givens" and sometimes few commonalities among academics' foundational beliefs, methodologies, and critical interests. His description of life within the research university today is a powerful one. Yet this same "dissensus" encompasses also the many divergent lifestyles, priorities, and institutional affiliations across the landscape *of* our profession. In Readings's dissensus model, profound differences of professional practice, critical methodology, worldview, etc. should be able to coexist within institutions while making no attempt to reach consensus; instead, they should value the strength of their thoughtful individuality. Given the crumbling of traditional notions of cultural homogeneity and practically any agreement on fixed or standard notions of value, Readings suggests that we imagine a community that is "heteronomous": "It does not pretend to have the power to name and determine itself; it insists that *the position of authority cannot be authoritatively occupied. . . .* Thought can only do justice to heterogeneity if it does not aim at consensus" (187, original emphasis). Readings imagines a university in which the social bond is one that "exceeds subjective consciousness" (186), and in which that bond is preserved as simultaneously a question and an obligation. I am broadening his call for such a dynamic of heteronomous co-existence to one that encompasses diversity among, not just within, institutions. There are attitudinal commonplaces and behavioral norms, and these also can be too rarely recognized and discussed. But the diversity of our profession is so very great that any sense of shared purpose and collegial respect among the various affiliations and sectors of the academy often seems impossible given the many radically disparate belief systems in existence, all invested with the heavy weight of "truth." Unless we learn how to approach critically our own position—to see the limitations of our own point of view—within that larger framework of diversity, we will continue to be severely hampered in our training of new professionals and at times even paralyzed in our interactions with each other.

Yet this no either/or situation. Even Readings admits that "To abandon consensus says nothing about limited or provisional forms of agreement and action, rather it says that the opposition of inclusion to exclusion (even a total inclusion of all humanity over and against the space alien) should not structure our notion of community, of sharing" (187). His model is a powerful and intriguing one, and his destabilizing of the inclusion/exclusion binary is important. But to forego consensus or homogeneity as an express or implicit goal does not mean necessarily abandoning an explicit recognition of overlap when it does exist or the necessity of continuing efforts toward coalition building and collegial coexistence. "Limited" and "provisional" do not capture adequately the manifold and multilayered ways that our practices as critics, teachers, and professionals are at times quite homogeneous while at other times strikingly divergent. After all, we may be a very diverse group of individuals, but we do, with surprising regularity, show up in a city and hotel on a given day and expect to find an academic conference there (with book exhibits and slide projectors in place). We may disagree vehemently on which poems to teach in class, but we do agree generally that poetry as a genre is worth attending to and teaching (unlike some who may think of higher education as only advanced vocational training). Indeed, we in the academy often seem oddly determined to dismiss or even demonize those closest at hand—within our own departments and our neighbor schools—while ignoring broader institutional and extra-professional groups and forces that can be far more divergent and even destructive in their beliefs concerning the work we do in the classroom, in our writing, and as public intellectuals. The most pressing and most difficult challenge facing "professional studies" today is valuing diversity and discussing it more openly, but at the same time sorting out commonalities and shared cultural beliefs, some of them laudable while others need challenging.

Thus it is worth musing for a moment on what "professional studies" means and can mean. I would like such studies to center on a rigorous honing of the same textual reading skills used to discuss the genres of literature, film, and culture but redirected to the text of our own profession. Indeed, it is a text that is more labyrinthine, multiplotted, and densely detailed than any novel by James Joyce or William Faulkner (and, at times, with some of the same plot lines). Indeed, it is one that has received some worthwhile critical scrutiny in recent years. In addition to Readings's *The University in Ruins,* books by Gerald Graff (*Professing Literature*), Terry Caesar (*Conspiring With Forms*), David Damrosch (*We Scholars*), James Phelan (*Beyond the Tenure Track*), Cary Nelson (*Manifesto of a Tenured Radical*), Michael Bérubé (*The Employment of English*), and J. Hillis Miller (*Black Holes*) offer superb insights into the particulars of employment, graduate training, and public intellectualism today. My collection of essays, *Professions: Conversations on the Future of Literary and Cultural Studies,* also captures some of the complexities of academic lifestyles, priorities, and affiliations at the turn of a new millennium. Yet there is still much interpretive and applied critical work to be done. While some have decried the quantity of work already published in the field of professional studies as exhaustive, I believe that we have barely scratched the surface of a multilayered and provocative text.

I agree with many of the above-mentioned commentators that active forms of *professionalization*—seminars, workshops, roundtables, etc.—are highly worthwhile components of professional studies as institutionalized in graduate programs today; "anti-professionalism," as Stanley Fish has pointed out in *Doing What Comes Naturally,* is simply a professional stance in itself—and a fairly unhelpful and even selfish one at that. But a larger question remains substantially unaddressed: what forms should professionalization take? Is it "descriptive" or is it "prescriptive," and if the latter, in what overtly revisionary ways? Is the outcome of professionalization a next generation of academics who are confident and authoritative or who are rigid and authoritarian? These questions seem to imply a blank-slate quality to the graduate student mind, one upon which programs inscribe positive or negative qualities. That is a condescending and simplistic construct. Certainly I saw some nascent, rather grim and rigid personality types among my fellow graduate students a dozen years ago, some of whom seem to have chosen this profession because of a covert desire to find a way of constructing an irrefutable argument, to learn how to *be* an authority, and to deploy that authority over a captive audience of students. But beyond such stark cases, I am also sure that the process of professionalization can bring out the best or worst aspects of complex personalities, characters, and work habits of professors-in-training. Even if we enter graduate school with the most supple minds and earnest desires to learn and talk about ideas, books, and a wide variety of texts, what information is passed along, what skills are exercised, and what professional behaviors and character traits are validated there?

Certain "nuts and bolts" topics clearly demand attention for professionals-in-training: the process by which one writes conference papers and gets them accepted, by which one produces articles and books and finds a publication venue for them, by which one gets a job and then tenure, and so on. These are well covered in a couple of books that I recommend highly: Heiberger and Vick's *The Academic Job Search Handbook* and Showalter et al.'s *The MLA Guide to the Job Search*. Yet there are subjective aspects of a successful career that are just as important to consider in any formal or informal discussion of our profession, ones that go beyond a "how-to" understanding of its mechanical aspects. "Why are we drawn to this profession and what do we expect from it?" are questions too infrequently asked of ourselves, students, and each other. What are the range of possibilities for research, teaching, service, and even administration—and ways of finding fulfillment through varying combinations of them—in a variety of institutional affiliations? What institutional norms or expectations are unacceptable and in need of radical revision, and what professional attitudes and behaviors are equally unacceptable and in need of revision?

One clear reason that our discussion of these issues has been so limited is that graduate school mentors can too often extrapolate from a narrow set of personally held goals and priorities and see them as natural or "real" for others. It is a common, human, ego-driven trait, and I would hardly claim to be guiltless in this respect. But I believe that in active and energetic conversation with others we can begin to learn about those tendencies and blind spots. In an outside review of this book, one of my two helpful readers suggested that the present chapter could be improved if I articulated "a clear vision of the ideal of intellectual work." In dialogue with my editor at the Ohio State University Press, I resisted defining "the" ideal because, in fact, one of my broadest points here is that we come to academic work for many reasons and with many and diverse ideals. We may be motivated to embark on a life in the academy because of a primary love of teaching and instructional activity, or because of a desire to do historical or archival work and write about our findings, or because we seek a community of supportive intellectuals and vibrant, daily interactions with other thinkers. For most of us, perhaps, our "ideal" is a particular combination of all of those and others. But I must remember always—and you should, too—that my balance, goals, and priorities are not "naturally" yours, and vice versa.

Whatever our primary motivational "ideal" or ideal balance, almost all of our work lives involve a myriad of tasks that include teaching, research, and collegiality, even though some of them may be difficult or highly uncomfortable for us. We must accept (or at least make our peace with) *all* of the necessary aspects of our work beyond any primary ideal or motivation, even as we seek a balance and a venue for our careers that meet as many of our needs as possible. Those ideals and balances may even change dramatically. You may find that a balance far different from the one that you projected as your "ideal" while in graduate school leads to a very fulfilling career. Or that a particular affiliation's priorities and its definition of the "ideal" balance are wholly incompatible with what you discover is your own. But certainly all the components of that balance—teaching, research, service, collegial community, and even administration—can be invigorating and intellectually dynamic parts of a multifaceted and enjoyable academic life. All have a wide range of possibilities and definitional parameters, ones too infrequently discussed. Admittedly, the following does not address many important issues, such as the need for a greater number of tenure-track jobs and the grave situation of underemployed adjuncts. Michael Bérubé's *The Employment of English* and Cary Nelson's *Manifesto of a Tenured Radical* discuss those and related topics with great insight. What I do offer in the coming pages are some thoughts and specific strategies for negotiating the many possible components of a career. Readers should mull them over and treat them with a healthy skepticism. While I draw widely on the experience base of similarly situated colleagues and friends, I take full responsibility for the suggestions I offer here. They clearly come out of my standpoint epistemology as they reflect my own context and set of evolving responses to it. At the very least, and perhaps at the very best, they should spark further discussion.

The Hierarchy of Affiliations

Let us first honestly address (before we can critically challenge, if we so desire) the real but often unacknowledged and rarely discussed hierarchy of jobs that exist in the worldviews of many academics. We are aware of the supposed "national hierarchy of colleges and universities, roughly correlated with the research reputations of their faculty members and their selectivity in admitting students" (Heiberger 10). Such hierarchical thinking is reinforced (and marketed) annually in the various lists of "best schools" (which are often based on some rather questionable sampling and data). But what we rarely talk about is how the same thinking affects/infects our own perceptions of where we should make our careers. What are implicitly defined as the best jobs—the ones that graduate students are often solely and expressly trained for—are those occupied by the faculty doing the training: ones at research schools. These positions involve relatively modest expectations of teaching (one, two, or occasionally three courses a semester) and high expectations of published research. As that balance shifts away from research and toward teaching, the "prestige" of the position sinks dramatically. This bias toward research as *the* value-determining component of our professional lives may reflect the base-level desires of some entering this profession who are drawn to it primarily in order to write and publish rather than to teach. Although I have no quarrel with anyone's base-level needs, it is possible that hierarchies of professional value among graduate students and aspiring professionals are at least shaped and reinforced by the values and biases of the faculty whom they regularly encounter. If few or no alternate perspectives and value systems are heard, then obviously the ones circulating in particular venues have at least the appearance of being true, natural, or real.

There is nothing real or true about them. Hierarchies of affiliation and the "prestige" level ascribed to jobs exist solely as conventions, as professional/social constructs. We should bring the same thorough skepticism to those constructs that we do to constructs of gender, race, and sexuality. While certainly there are exploitative situations in which faculty are asked to do far too much work for too little pay or are allowed no job security as they race across town to teach part-time at several schools, those extremes should not obscure the fact that *there is no real or true correlation between the teaching/research balance of a position and its inherent value*. Yes, a particular balance may be more valuable to a specific individual because of her or his own needs and desires, but we should not generalize from what should be a personal decision to any designation of "real" or "true" value. Unless we begin by admitting and remembering that fact, none of the discussion that follows will be of use.

In thinking about (or upon accepting) a position at an institution unlike that of one's training, one must suspend, to the extent possible, any naturalized judgments about that position's inherent worth. The same is equally true for how we should approach positions that carry very high prestige value. It is far more important for us to choose wisely rather than conventionally and to thrive in positions that are appropriate for our individual priorities and abilities. I have seen the disastrous consequences of individuals accepting positions at research schools when they clearly should have been making their careers at teaching schools. And I certainly have seen the bitterness of individuals employed at the latter who still feel, many years later, that they deserve "better."

Teaching

If we *can* see the range of common teaching loads in our profession, when they are appropriately balanced with other professional expectations, as ones without intrinsic value beyond that to which we ascribe them, we can at least begin to discuss the trade-offs and possibilities for career fulfillment that do exist outside of the few jobs available at research institutions. The variety of institutional expectations regarding teaching is dramatic. Some schools demand that its most illustrious senior faculty teach only one course a semester (or even one course a year in a very few cases); others require all faculty to teach four (or very rarely even five) courses a semester. Some adjunct faculty, whose very particular and often extreme job situations fall outside the scope of this book, sometimes teach far more than that in order to patch together a minimal economic existence. Those superexploited faculty deserve our collective support for moving them toward job security and equitable pay and benefits.

But as much as the range above would seem to lend itself to a simplistic equation between the quantity of teaching and the quality of a particular position (the more teaching, the worse the job, because the more "work" one has to do), such a reading needs considerable complication. For one thing, any denigration of teaching or perception of it as an obstacle *to* our work should be regarded as bias against what is perhaps the most important activity in which we engage as professionals. Indeed, a far more important consideration is whether or not a specific institution and department administration creates a situation in which we can teach well and that appropriately recognizes and rewards the teaching that we do. Yes, sometimes *more* teaching can mean *less* time to devote to teaching individual classes, which may then suffer, but the simple raw number of courses taught each semester says little about the number of students one might have (three sections of forty-five students each is hardly "better" than four sections of twenty-five students each), the number of preparations in a given semester (the difference between two sections of two different courses and one section of four different courses is dramatic), the type of courses assigned (including the number of writing courses), the amount of written feedback required (some colleges require copious narrative reports on students as well as grades), and the amount of flexibility one has in choosing the courses that one will teach (including how many different and new preparations are required each semester). Because we have often been so fixated on those raw numbers—4/4, 3/3, 2/2—we often fail to discuss the obvious fact that teaching loads can be considerably less onerous if one avoids teaching new courses until the subject matter coincides with research interests and if one schedules courses carefully on two or three days a week rather than four or five days a week. Thus for all job candidates considering positions at teaching or research schools, it is imperative to reflect upon when and to what extent one has agency in a given situation. If one has the freedom substantially to choose one's own teaching schedule (time of day, day of the week, type of course and number of preparations), then what may seem to be a less desirable position can be revalued and discovered to be far more desirable than conventional wisdom would suggest. The reverse is also true: if you are obliged forever and always to teach a certain set of courses and on an inconvenient schedule, you may find out that a lower raw number is not intrinsically better than a higher raw number.

Finally, even the diction involved in the commonly used phrase "teaching load" needs critical scrutiny. Institutions that self-define as teaching schools usually pride themselves on the emphasis they place on meeting student needs, and they usually reward good teaching appropriately, valuing it centrally (though rarely exclusively) as a component of tenure, promotion, and salary increase processes. Being affiliated with such a student-centered institution should never be regarded as a clear and self-evident "burden." One might decide that teaching working-class students at a community college is far more important than teaching at a research institution, however the larger profession ascribes relative value to both. Another individual might locate greater personal value in research rather than teaching. Those are decisions based on an individual's chosen professional self-identity; the value of a given balance among the various components of a career discussed here is neither real nor natural.

Research

Scholarship and publication also demand revisiting and reevaluating; they, too, should never be regarded as a simple, self-evident component of our professional lives. The wide diversity of research paths and the many choices that active scholars, writers, and researchers must make are also too rarely discussed in graduate programs and professional studies venues. Such diversity involves institutional expectations, which can vary widely, and also concerns the type of research and writing the academic wishes to perform and the audience he/she wishes to reach.

Institutions should always render as transparent as possible their research expectations and definitions. It is reasonable that a given university would require a book for tenure—or even more than that—if it states that requirement up front and then makes the meeting of it possible through an appropriate teaching assignment and expenditure of resources in support of necessary travel, equipment, etc. But if any fuzziness about expectations lingers, then the job candidate or new junior professor should proactively search out information to fill in the blanks to the extent possible. Often university handbooks and written departmental guidelines will provide considerable information about the quantity and quality of the research required for tenure and promotion to associate and later full professor. Some handbooks and guidelines may be vague or poorly written, and even more clarification may be needed through meetings with senior faculty and administrators, but it is also surprising how much self-willed ignorance exists in our profession. Academics too frequently either assume they already know what they have to do for career advancement and proceed with misinformation in hand, or perhaps have already decided what they *will* do and then hide from the fact that their goals and projects do not meet institutional requirements. This almost always leads to disaster. Even regarding what seems to be the most self-evident category—a monograph for tenure—it is imperative that the professor discover exactly what type of press, for example, is recognized as legitimate. While there may be considerable leeway, there is also a lot of information that can be gleaned from colleagues and administrators about past practices and previous valuations of presses and forms of publication or research.

Whatever the institution's requirements are, those *must be* the minimum goals and first priorities of the academic interested in remaining at his/her current institution and thriving there. I have known academics who were told explicitly that for tenure they needed to publish a scholarly book with a university press, but who decided instead to devote all of their time to writing a textbook or introductory volume on a neglected author for an undergraduate audience, and who were later fired because of their decision. The projects to which they devoted themselves may have been very worthwhile, but the decisions that they made were inappropriate and ultimately self-destructive given their context.

At some colleges and universities a wider variety of genres and types of writing may be recognized as legitimate for promotion purposes (information that should be considered as any candidate mulls over a job offer). Besides scholarly monographs (which can be very differently valued depending upon the press involved) and articles (which are also variously valued depending upon whether or not they appear in refereed journals or elsewhere), there are also book reviews, editing projects (whether essay collections or special issues of journals), encyclopedia-type entries, creative writing, popular cross-over writing (such as articles in newspapers or popular periodicals), and textbooks. Not all of these "count" at every institution, and the individual academic must seek information about what will or will not positively affect one's tenure and promotion chances. In fact, some may actually count against one (demonstrating misplaced priorities or even a "weak mind" in some scholars' opinions). After being promoted to full professor one can perhaps choose freely without worrying about consequences (though even then pay raises will no doubt be based on the same sets of distinctions), but while one is still "in" the personnel process one cannot ignore contextual belief systems without risking disaster.

Other forms of diversity across the landscapes—geographical, ideological, and behavioral—of our profession also deserve mention. Diversity of access to libraries and research materials, of monetary support for travel, summer research, and equipment can affect profoundly our research and writing lives, and all should be part of the research a job candidate does as he/she considers an affiliation or a career path. But another form of diversity to which I must return time and again is that of our own actions and degrees of responsibility. In my next chapter I will discuss more fully how many of us can better define and schedule our goals and projects so that we keep our commitments to ourselves, our colleagues, and our institutions. But it is worth remembering that colleges and universities always have limited—sometimes even very scarce—resources to devote to supporting research, and that if we squander those resources or fail to complete funded projects, then it is fully understandable that those resources will be given to someone else who will use them more effectively. We have to choose wisely those projects to which we will devote ourselves and make sure their completion is possible. Others may have been denied funding because we were funded, others' careers may be jeopardized if we renege on our commitments, and the morale of a community may suffer because of our contribution to a culture of irresponsibility. Thus even our research, which may be conducted in solitary fashion, always affects the durability and strength of a larger social web.

And this web may include strands linking us very directly to our colleagues and in innovative ways to our students. We are only beginning as a profession to explore the possibilities of conducting and rewarding collaborative work, but as Patricia Lonchar-Fite notes in her contribution to the SCMLA mentioned earlier, "If we are serious about attaining the balance Hall discusses without mortgaging our professional and personal futures, we must stop setting up a dichotomy between teaching and research and between individual activity and collaboration" (6). Some institutions reward such work and others do not; sometimes we can challenge and alter our institution's valuation of collaborative work, and sometimes we will discover many obstacles. But in all cases, one must seek out information very aggressively, especially if one is a junior faculty contemplating an investment of time and energy in a form of work that may or may not be valued highly by a given college or university.

While I will discuss burnout at greater length in chapter 3, I add another facet to the useful admonition above regarding the unnecessary dichotomy between teaching and research: intellectual isolation, methodological anachronism, and professional provinciality among teaching academics are never in the interests of the students of those academics. While we may like to think that our teaching can be superb even if we never publish or otherwise participate in wider professional discussions, rarely is that possible. The most vibrant teachers are those who fully engage in the intellectual flow and excitement of their fields. The worst are clueless about a rapidly changing professional conversation. We may be kind and supportive teachers, but we are still failing to fulfill our pedagogical responsibilities if we do not remain current in our fields of teaching interest. The passing along of anachronistic information should be no more acceptable in the humanities than it would be in the natural sciences.

Service

Like teaching, service is often considered a burden, something to be shouldered necessarily at times but shifted as often as possible to someone else. This needs to be rethought as we begin to see ourselves not in isolation but as community members, and to consider the diverse ways in which we can act as intellectuals. Service can be yet another aspect of our careers in which we find intense fulfillment, or it *can be* frustrating and burdensome.

Certainly the diversity of what service entails and the actual expectation of types and amount of service in institutions varies dramatically. Here as above, candidates and faculty members should be told what is expected of them, and if any questions or lack of clarity remains, then the academic should aggressively seek out all necessary information. The term "service" usually comprises several possible fields of commitment: department, college or school, university, and off-campus community. Often, service at all levels is required for tenure and promotion; but precisely where and how we devote our energies can be an important choice. As elsewhere, it is important to research the limits of one's agency in a given situation: when can one say "no" to a request to serve on a committee outside one's area of interest or refuse to take on a project with a particularly heavy time commitment when other responsibilities already press? Colleagues and administrators should be able to provide such information, but remember also that when we turn down an assignment, it is usually pressed on someone else. Thus in saying no, it may be communally responsible to offer to work on a different service project that is more in line with one's own interest and expertise. Simply "getting out of service" as much as possible is a very uncollegial activity.

Indeed, many service opportunities are not burdensome but intellectually invigorating. Involvement in curriculum and program reform, in planning and assessment, in institutional governance, in hiring and promotion committees, in scheduling lectures and arranging colloquia—these all provide extraordinary opportunities to put our theories into practice, to *act* in ways that reflect our critical stances and beliefs. If approached with the right attitude and under efficacious collegial circumstances, service can be an integral and exciting part of our work as intellectuals. In reading, interacting with, and responding to the very complex texts of our institutions—which is what most service *is*, after all—we are not being pulled away from our work, we are doing our work as cultural/textual critics. If we define service as somehow opposed to our work, then we have deliberately chosen a professional self-identity that is neither collegially responsible nor even intellectually nuanced.

Beyond its inherent vitality and intellectual content, some service actually abets our other work. For example, I have chosen to involve myself in advising and administration in my department and college, not only because I consider such activity intrinsically interesting and as textually involved as any project of literary analysis but also because it is traded for teaching responsibilities, as it is at many other universities. I have never done less work thereby, often much more, but certainly the work has been more diverse than would otherwise be the case. Administration and advising, if involving such "reassigned time," may in some cases make clearer and more predictable demands on one's daily schedule than class preparation, grading, and active instruction. The difference in the *type* of energy that I have expended has meant that I have had more energy to devote to my research. However, others have found advising duties, for example, to be an endless vacuum into which time and energy are drawn, so such a tradeoff may not be efficacious for everyone; it depends upon one's ability to schedule, prioritize, and contain the worries that go along with such duties. Knowing our own abilities, tendencies, and limits, we have to choose wisely.

The same is true for commitments outside of our institutional homes. I have found my community service to be one of the most important components of my personal and professional life. Even if only for one or two hours a week, the work that I have done with social service organizations has helped keep the walls that sometimes surround an "ivory tower" existence from going up in hard and fast ways. I have had to choose such work (to lead a support group for an AIDS organization and to do in-service training on sensitivity to issues of sexual diversity) carefully so that I know it will fit into an already busy schedule but have found such activity to be an integral part of an active, multifaceted intellectual life. Indeed, such work outside of our institutions can remind us often of our own limitations; in making ourselves a part of organizations and processes in which we are novices, we remain aware of the boundaries of our knowledge and authority. Community service can thus play a vital role in helping us "own" our self-identities.

Finally, one reason that service is so often perceived as (and actually can be) burdensome has more to do with group dynamics than it does with the task of the committee to which one is assigned. As I will reiterate in my chapter on collegiality, we must be more respectful of each other's time. Clear agendas, commitments to efficient meetings, a careful parceling out of duties, and a responsible fulfillment of those duties are all vital for a well-functioning committee or group project. On the other hand, lateness, irresponsible behavior, and long-winded and self-indulgent monologues can be very destructive. Unless we "own" the ways that our individual behaviors (and, specifically, self-indulgences) can affect others, we will always be a profession riven by anger and resentment. Institutional expectations of service can be oppressive, but our actions toward each other in the process of fulfilling our service commitment can also be oppressive, sometimes in the simple passive-aggressive way of not showing up to a meeting or not returning an important e-mail. Rarely do we seem willing to admit or address that fact. My next chapter will discuss planning and scheduling possibilities that can help groups as well as individuals better articulate and meet goals.

Collegiality

Indeed, we too rarely discuss our communal behavior and support systems as an integral part of our professional existences. Because I feel this is such an important topic, I will devote most of my fourth chapter to it. But I do want to mention briefly here that any consideration of a possible career affiliation or even articulation of a professional self-identity should place collegiality at the heart of one's work life. Some institutions with very attractive teaching loads and benefit packages are, in fact, vicious places, torn by internal struggles and dominated by some angry, suspicious individuals. That ethos can perhaps be changed, but such changes can take a great deal of time and energy. Collegial dynamics are part of the text of a department and a career. Job candidates, in particular, should be very well-informed—should aggressively seek out all possible information—about any group or institution with which they are considering a daily affiliation. Here as elsewhere, ignorance—so often self-willed—is never blissful for very long.

Administration

As an academic it is important to consider both the ways that administrators will impact one's professional life and the ways that work in administration may be part of that life. Regarding the former, job candidates or new colleagues should seek out all information about the attitudes and agendas of administrators—department chairs, deans, and provosts—to whom they may link their career. These are the individuals who will help determine whether or not one is employed six years after an initial job offer. And beyond seeking out information as one considers a position, after taking a job, one should (to the extent possible) establish a solid working relationship with administrators. As Cathy Davidson points out in an essay quoted earlier, the "us/them" attitude that seems to structure faculty/administration relationships is far too simplistic to account for the ways in which our lives are conjoined and our professional existences coextensive. Yes, administrations can be oppressive, but this cannot be said of all of them. It is vital when disagreements with administrators arise that we research what differences in priorities and goals help account for those disagreements, where and how we can exercise agency in changing others' opinions, and where and when our own goals and opinions should change.

In thus "humanizing" administrators we may discover that an administrative career path is an attractive one for us to consider. As I have suggested throughout this chapter, institutions are texts that are as multilayered and complex as that of any novel. We may decide that those institutional texts are ones to which we can devote our analytical and creative energies with passion. And even if we simply admit that this is a possibility (and a valid choice for any intellectual to make), we thereby continue to complicate our perspective on our colleagues and their professional lives. I have heard far too many scholars deride administrators as "failed" researchers. It is those sneering scholars who are usually "failing" intellectually by oversimplifying. Administrative work can offer profound opportunities for meaningful, intellectual action as important as, or even more important than, the production of a scholarly monograph. Furthermore, administration that is devoted to creating an environment of intellectual vitality in a department or university has an impact that is stunningly exponential, for the professional lives of numerous faculty are enhanced and invigorated. Individual successes are often dependent upon the successful working together of a group, in which successful administration plays a vital role. This is a part of the text of our professional lives that is far too often ignored.

~

In charting all the above components of a career and our collective professional lives, I am urging each of us to view critically the texts of our self-identities and the contexts in which those self-identities are expressed and lived. That movement between text and context is the only mechanism by which we can also become aware of both our potentials for agency and the necessity of accepting some of the unchangeable aspects of our careers. In charting those forces and factors, I cannot emphasize enough the utility of and invigoration provided by a process of active career planning, through and obviously well beyond the professional statement explored in the previous chapter. To think not only in terms of the next month and year but also with an eye toward the more distant future is essential if we are going to sustain our sense of intellectual commitment as well as our equanimity when faced with the inevitable turmoils of our professional lives.

That focus on the long term clearly runs against the grain of some popular self-help advice to "live in the moment." To be sure, the intense joys of our teaching, service, research, and collegial engagement should be savored as they occur, and it is a mistake to concentrate so exclusively on what may or may not happen five years from now that today's successes are downplayed and short-term goals and pressing needs are neglected. But unfortunately, when we live substantially "in the moment," we too often fail to commit to long-term, very slow processes; furthermore, we may act and react out of immediate feeling and with little or no reflection. I have seen the destructive consequences of individuals within departments, professional organizations, and faculty governance groups who live wholly within the moment of their own anger and sense of wounded pride.

But if we as individuals (and groups) can act and react with reference not only to the present moment but also our long-term goals for interpersonal relations, a collegial environment, the success of collaborative projects, and, yes, individual achievement, then our momentary feelings are tempered by our memory of other, mitigating factors and forces. In effect, an active process of career planning that involves all the previously mentioned components prods us to *remember* both synchronic and diachronic complexity when one or the other seems momentarily paramount. To remember the different perspectives and goals of our colleagues and administrators, to remember our own research goals when distractions press, to remember our goals for collegiality when our feathers are ruffled in a department meeting, to remember our goals for teaching when a possible appointment would take us out of the classroom completely—these are the payoffs of career planning and of textualizing those plans in professional statements and the forms of concrete, even visualizable, processing that I will explore in my next chapter.

Yet, it is equally important in any search for sustainable equanimity to retain flexibility in our plans. New opportunities will arise and new personalities will enter our professional lives. Our priorities in balancing our professional and personal lives will change dramatically over time. A career plan must be an organic document in which we allow for that metamorphosis and those shifting balances. We must remain active readers of our professional contexts and writers of our own professional texts. And this is why "careerism" is such a flawed formula. Its emphasis on individual quantitative "achievement" is too simplistic, narrow, and atomized for it to lead to anything other than profound and accelerating anxieties. Success cannot be quantified or reduced to achievement in only one of the component parts of a professional life described above. A happy and balanced professional life includes a successful negotiating and renegotiating of all or most of the above; setbacks or disappointments in one area can thereby always be offset by a sense of continuing accomplishment in others.

My final major point is that what is true at the individual level is also true at the group, departmental, or institutional level. If individuals self-disclose and openly discuss their professional self-identities, so, too, should institutions. If individual professionals should remain balanced and aware of the many components of a thriving intellectual existence, so, too, should departments. Individuals need short-, medium-, and long-term goals; so do academic communities.

Many in our profession react with understandable cynicism toward strategic planning processes. They see the documents generated in such processes as destined for a file in an administrator's office and forgotten soon after the completion of a process that may be timeconsuming and labor intensive. That may very well be how such documents are received and used at the college or university level. But that does not need to be how groups of colleagues use them. While Bill Readings has analyzed the hollow rhetoric of excellence in university public relations in recent years, departments do not have to see the planning process as a hollow one. An open discussion of group goals and priorities, of balances among the components discussed above, of desires for cohesiveness and respect for diversity, and of individual contributions to collective successes is vital to a process of making functional rather than dysfunctional the state of dissensus in which we find ourselves. Just as individual career plans must remain open to change and thoughtful metamorphosis, so too must collective plans. Individual plans can be made untenable by careerism and a overly narrow focus on quantitative achievement in only one of the many parts of a professional existence; likewise, a department can focus so narrowly on "publication" that it is rendered anxious and is plagued by anger. All these issues deserve overt discussion in planning sessions and other venues.

A flexible but well-thought-out departmental plan and statement of self-identity should be a key component of hiring and acculturation. It plays a vital role in the honest exchange of information that must take place as job candidates mull over a possible association with a department and as a department searches for the "best fit" among many applicants. Without such self-awareness on the part of candidates and institutions, and an energetic and forthright exchange of information, disaster looms in the form of deep rifts among faculty, terrible mismatches and anxieties over institutional priorities and wildly divergent individual abilities, and a general culture of dishonesty and suspicion. That is how snakes come to inhabit our proverbial snakepits.

None of the above is meant to suggest that individual academics or the departments they collectively form exercise agency outside of the boundaries and influences of larger institutional limitations and priorities. If a university defines "excellence" as a book for tenure, it will be difficult for a department to define "success" in dramatically different terms, especially in the short run. But there is certainly no reason why a department or group of faculty cannot set as its medium- or long-term goal a concert-ed effort to challenge and moderate that inflexible university definition (or even make it more rigorous, if that is the well-thought-out group goal). But only by openly discussing and actively negotiating priorities and goals can effective group efforts be mounted and shared beliefs be identified.

Dissensus does not have to mean distress. All the above are meant to open up a new discussion on the individual and group level of the text of professional success. How do we define it, what are its component parts, and how can we create a culture in which individual and group accom-plishments are nurtured? I have my own thoughts on success that I will share in my coda to this book, but I recognize that it will be differently defined and its components balanced variously depending upon one's own personality, interests, institutional affiliation, and contextual demands. Yet simply to denaturalize our common, received professional definition of success—a "prestigious" job and series of high-profile publications—would itself be a dramatic achievement. It would open up for critical scrutiny our preconceptions about the value we attribute to an affiliation, a press, a form of publication, and the activities to which we might devote ourselves professionally. It might even disrupt our profession's current fas-cination with narrowly defined "stardom" and reveal that construct to be meaningful on only the most hollow and intellectually suspicious levels.

chapter three
. . . .

Process

*b*UILDING ON MY discussion in the last two chapters, I want to turn now to what we *do* with our acceptance of "ownership." If, as I suggest, we can more forthrightly examine our own professional needs and career goals, and if we can also probe and understand the institutional constraints with which we have to contend in our careers, how do we use that base of knowledge as a starting point for action and achievement? In the coming pages, I wil expand my notion of "text" to include that of "process." Can we analyze and better understand our own planning, scheduling, and work habits, also with an eye toward a greater degree of ownership? I am not talking about "control" over careers or daily work lives, but I am suggesting that we can usefully discuss when and where we can affect outcomes profoundly and how we can exercise agency when possible and appropriate, rather than feel overwhelmed, stressed, or burned out. The following discussion focuses largely on research and writing processes—since they are the most literally textual forms of work we engage in—but the concepts I discuss here have an applicability well beyond research; they apply to pedagogical, communal, and a wide variety of institutional processes as well.

Indeed, the same overall care required to produce publishable research is required for a host of other goals and processes, including those that are collective rather than individual. Any group of people coming together to address the most profound inequities or effect the most radical changes to an institution or system must be able to articulate thoughtfully their shared goals, plan carefully to achieve those goals, and manage their time wisely so that all component parts of their plan are accomplished. Thus nothing that I say in this chapter or elsewhere in this book is meant to extol competition or to pit colleague against colleague. Instead, I hope it will encourage a *culture* of support for goal setting and achievement, and *(micro)systems* of encouragement, dialogue, and discussion on effective teaching, service, and scholarship. As groups of academics, we should approach with enthusiasm the processes, as well as value highly the products, of our work. Those processes of collegial support, debate, and interaction are far too often derided or dismissed.

Indeed, there is something about our work—so often conceived of as monadistic, even mutually antagonistic—that mitigates against this valuing of process, especially collective process. I remember once after completing a very energetic, if somewhat exhausting, committee process—of interviewing dozens of candidates for four jobs at the MLA convention, discussing the merits of each candidate, and arriving at a tentative ranking of choices for the positions—I attended a multi-institutional "executive committee" meeting at the very end of the conference. I entered the room, still filled with excitement over my department's hiring plans, sat down, and mentioned to another committee member that I just "loved process." He looked rather grim and skeptical, responding that he didn't understand "process" as it manifested itself in the academy; in fact, he went on to say that he couldn't even think of any viable or valuable processes among academics. I was stunned. He was a senior member of a prestigious department that hired every year; he had been a frequent member of committees that tenured and promoted (or decided not to); and he had selected panel topics, papers, and nominees for the very committee on which we both were serving (as we, in fact, did again over the next hour). Processes, both individual and collective, are part of our everyday professional life. We may not like their outcomes or dynamics, but they go on all the time. If we feel strongly about their dynamics or outcomes, then it is incumbent upon us to engage in a process of changing them, if they can be changed. But it is far too easy simply to sneer at them. Groups of academics are not hopelessly befuddled or antagonistic toward each other unless they choose those performances (and continuously choose not to challenge those performances). Processes, carefully discussed, committed to, managed, and often reflected upon, can be enormously enjoyable if we decide to approach them in that way. Cynicism about processes often serves only as an excuse for our refusal to participate or our unproductive participation in them.

Cynicism mystifies me; it is at best a sloppy reading strategy, a formula-driven textual response (and at worst a cover for anger and even more destructive tendencies). And I am not alone in seeking and seeing alternatives. Helpful books abound on how we process events and information in passively or actively destructive ways, including David Burns's *Feeling Good*, Philip McGraw's *Life Strategies*, and Matthew McKay et al.'s *When Anger Hurts*. Similarly, some excellent works offer concrete strategies on time management and, specifically, the dissertation-writing process. Among the standouts are Joan Bolker's *Writing Your Dissertation in Fifteen Minutes a Day* and, for a more general audience, Jeff Davidson's *The Complete Idiot's Guide to Managing Your Time*. I wish I had had such books to consult for general advice during my dissertation-writing process, but since I did not, I began to develop and hone my own planning, processing, and time management techniques. Some of my ideas are similar to what I found later in those books and related ones, some not. Beyond how my suggestions here may occasionally dovetail with those of other writers, my purpose is certainly broader: a "meta" discussion on the how's and why's concerning planning and processing, and, specifically, some of the process-related payoffs for those entering or employed in the academy. In their own guide to "process"—*The Academic Job Search Handbook*—Mary Heiberger and Julia Vick note that despite "their heavy workloads, academics have more freedom to structure their own time than practically anyone else in the economy. For some people, this is the great advantage of the career path; for others, it is a source of stress" (11). What I hope to do is offer you a few practical ways to reduce that stress.

Frankly, I plan, process, and manage my time carefully because that is how I *compress* and thereby intensely *express* my professional life in the most invigorating and enjoyable ways possible. As I will discuss in my coda to this book, I perhaps read Walter Pater at too young an age—early adolescence—but certainly I have long taken very seriously his injunction to "burn always with [a] hard, gemlike flame" (189). Focusing intensely on planning and processing is how I personally achieve that degree of energetic expression. It may sound anxiety-driven and stressful, but (unless I am in deep denial) it is not. Indeed, I have found that careful attention to processing and time management is how I best deal with stressful situations, as it allows me to sort out to the best of my abilities what is possible and impossible, what I can and cannot affect and effect. Not only does this emphasis on processing repay me with a sense of professional accomplishment, but it also allows me considerable time to enjoy my personal life. Unlike some, I know well when my work day is over. Part of the textuality of process is its beginning, middle, and most importantly, its end.

But as goal-driven as this may seem, much of the pleasure of planning, processing, and time management lies not in their end products—publication or project completion—it is derived from the nourishment—intellectual, communal, and professional—provided by the processes themselves. We all know (or should know by now) that we may complete professional tasks to the best of our abilities, "play by all of the rules," so to speak, even overachieve and push ourselves to extremes, and still be denied the book contract we have been working for, the position we have applied for, or the raise that we feel we deserve. If we tie our senses of professional payoff *only* to a desired reception of the end product of a process, then we are setting ourselves up for disappointment, perhaps even a state of bitterness or burnout.

This is how an attention to "process" can help reduce stress, how "burning" with that gem-like flame does not lead necessarily to burnout. To de-naturalize, to meta-theorize, and textualize "process" allows us considerable agency in redefining its payoffs, to remember always to glean profound intellectual pleasures from completing the various steps toward the product, as well as from our sense of accomplishment in having created the product, if only for ourselves. Concretely put, I cannot know if the words that I am writing at this moment will ever appear in any form of print other than that which comes out of my computer. Honestly, I cannot even be sure of that product since my hard drive may crash and these words may never appear anywhere other than the gray screen upon which they are materializing as I write. But I can decide that this act of creation, this thinking through of ideas as they move from conscious and subconscious thought through my fingers and onto the screen is enough to satisfy and sustain me, even if the unfortunate were to occur. I, like many of my readers, have chosen my career because the thinking through of complexities and the offering of thoughtful interpretations of and responses to compelling questions fascinate me. We engage in that activity continuously during the processes of researching, writing, revising, and discussing our past, current, and future projects. We do it as individuals engaging in research processes and as groups engaging in strategic planning processes. Those processes—and especially the intellectual activity and occasion for dialogue that they allow—must be more explicitly valued, must be recognized as professional "goods" in and of themselves. We simply do not have to have a specific *reaction* to the products of our processes for those processes to have been worthwhile.

This in no way means that we dispense with highly concrete goals. The discussion that our research, for example, both enters and attempts to alter is most broadly based when our words are disseminated through print and other widely accessed media. This is why publication is required for tenure and promotion and is an end product that should not be wholly ignored even when we remind ourselves of the joy of the process of research itself. Unpublished research simply does not contribute to professional conversations as widely, credibly, and accessibly as published research does (colleagues cannot access our ideas at all if they remain private or disseminated only to classes). By planning carefully we can maximize our chances of reaching the widest audience appropriate for our ideas. And certainly if one of our overarching goals is job security, or tenure, then to ignore a concrete requirement for it, such as the publication of a number of articles or a book manuscript, is to court disaster.

In much of this chapter I offer advice that is unabashedly directive and that is intended to provoke response, interpretation, and perhaps significant modification. Some of my talking points—building blocks—may seem simplistic upon first reading, but they are necessary as parts of processes, and their lack of completion—as simple, even simple-minded, as they are—often means that later steps are impossible. What I offer here has worked for me, and it may work for you, but I look forward to hearing about the successes and diverse strategies of others. Indeed, and as I indicate throughout this book, such an exchange of professional ideas and scripts is one of the broadest and most fascinating processes in which we are all engaged and by which we can be intellectually invigorated.

Talking Points on Textualizing Process

1. We should work carefully with the most literal "texts" of time: calendars, daybooks, planners, etc.

As we begin to approach the generation of short-, medium-, and long-term plans and textualize the processes that they involve, the first step is to schedule adequate time in which to engage in that process of generation, in which to consider carefully, write out precisely, and revise thoughtfully our goals and plans, before committing ourselves fully to them. We should never hide from inflexible constraints. First, we might research when and how our time is already limited and/or committed in clear and unchangeable ways (by the beginnings of semesters, by meetings, conferences, and vacation plans) and interact physically with the text of the calendar: marking off days or weekends that are already devoted to other demands, priorities, or interests. Barring unseen emergencies or unexpected demands that may arise, time is subdividable, regular, and predictable. In effectively textualizing and owning process, it is imperative that we know from the outset how many days, even hours, we can devote to a specific process—research, pedagogical, or communal—in the coming weeks, months, or even year or more. That difficult delineation—best "guess," perhaps—is fundamental to all other work we will do. The fact that we can never "know" definitively or precisely how much time we have to work with should never deter us from striving to know approximately, tentatively, or to the best of our abilities.

It is also vital, as we begin to work on processing, that we draw carefully on our knowledge of our past actions and abilities. If we approach our professional self-identities as texts, the text of our own past behaviors is one that we should read with particular care (both to learn from and perhaps work on). After years of writing in graduate school and as an academic, I know, for example, that I write rough drafts at about one to two pages per hour. It varies at times, but that has always been my average writing speed and is an approximation that I can use as I generate schedules. I also know that I usually revise at about half that speed, and that I generally revise manuscripts four and occasionally five or more times, depending on their complexity. This textualizing of my work habits allows me to plan with some accuracy about when I can reasonably expect to complete a review, an essay, even a book, as I work with a calendar. While mine may seem an extreme case of self-textualization, we certainly all use intuitive estimations of the time needed for tasks and projects every day—when to leave for the office given traffic patterns, when to begin grading a set of papers in order to return them to students by the following week. I am suggesting here that we acknowledge and more forthrightly use that base of acquired knowledge and the tools of calendars and day planners as we interact with all aspects of our professional self-identities.

This is far from science, but I am urging that we think as precisely as possible about what we can reasonably expect to accomplish and by when. We may think that by setting vague, ambitious, admirable, but unrealistic goals that we are challenging ourselves, but really we are running some serious risks. If I have vague plans that I cannot live up to, the slippage in my commitments and completion dates will have a domino-like effect rippling perhaps through years of my career. I will feel frustrated and perhaps despairing; others may be angry and always suspicious afterward, if they were depending upon my work. I may even damage forever my relationship with my institution, which may have entrusted me with funding or required a certain level of achievement for tenure or promotion. It is far better to schedule our goals and work toward them honestly and accurately rather than plan vaguely to achieve the herculean and then fail miserably. I always challenge myself, but I always try to schedule in such a way that I meet minimum performance standards, fulfill agreements with others, and build in accomplishable micro-goals so I can feel a sense of achievement as I move through long, arduous processes.

I have years broadly mapped out in advance, with tentative deadlines penciled in and intermediate goals noted. My research and writing plan is scheduled explicitly, week by week, for the next year. But most important, all my days that are devoted to professional tasks are scheduled hour by hour for the next month. Yes, there are surprises, and my schedule almost inevitably breaks down and must be altered. Effectively textualizing process means that we must return to our texts often, rewriting and revising them as necessary. But you will be amazed at how much writing, reading, grading, teaching, and socializing can be condensed into a day if you plan carefully. This may sound like abject workaholism, *but I always stop working at 5* P.M. In fact, effective scheduling means I have more time—all evenings and much of the weekend—for the personal activities that I love.

2. But to schedule effectively, we must break down all projects into component parts and schedule them accordingly.

Every process has internal elements into which it can be subdivided and external influences on it to which it must respond or which it must take into account. Books are dividable into chapters, pages, and paragraphs. Tenure processes are divisible into vita items and the activities of teaching, communal work, and collegial responsibility. Decisions on whom to hire or what format a new graduate program will take are divisible into an articulation of goals by committees and then a series of decisions regarding the best way to meet those goals. All of these can be done gradually and methodically, with one eye on the date of desired completion and the other on the necessary steps—even very small ones—that must be taken today in order to move toward that completion.

It is impossible to anticipate all the various difficulties and smaller tasks that will arise as processes move forward, but just because we cannot anticipate everything does not mean that we should avoid trying to anticipate as many as possible. Recognizing that the unanticipated will inevitably occur means we can build a buffer into our schedules and processes. If we know that we are going to have an unproductive day occasionally, we can schedule our writing so that we have a cushion. Indeed, I never schedule so tightly that a missed day or bout with the flu will wreak total havoc on my schedule. Of course for some that cushion becomes an enabler of procrastination; my own tendency is to challenge myself by minimizing my scheduling of buffer time. I don't want to think that I can "blow off today" and not have to worry about it. I want to know that when I complete my work today—my chapter of reading, my five pages of writing, my 20 pages of grading—I have already protected this evening and this weekend for personal pursuits and necessary "down time."

3. Articulate micro-goals that allow you to monitor and build on your successes.

If we have broken down our projects or goals into their component parts and scheduled their completion so we know how and by when our processes will be completed, then we are offered daily checks on whether or not we are, in fact, succeeding. As discussed above, I have decided that the vitality of engaging in the process is, for me and at this point in my career, the most significant payoff of all. Therefore the achievement of those micro-goals—proof of that vitality—constitutes an "end" in itself, not simply a means to an end.

Every day I find some form of scheduled accomplishment to feel sustained by, even if that goal is something as small as reading ten pages or revising thoroughly a page of a manuscript. And beyond such continual nourishment, the constant monitoring of smaller units of progress toward larger forms of achievement, means that schedules can be adjusted and readjusted as necessary. Planning and scheduling does not mean inscribing anything in stone. Returning to and adjusting a schedule is also part of the vitality of the process. Indeed, simply fine-tuning a schedule is often enough to re-energize us and help us move past the moments of inertia that we all occasionally encounter.

4. We must work responsibly to meet all self-imposed and agreed-upon deadlines.

This brings us to our ownership responsibilities. If we lie to ourselves that skipping our responsibilities today will have no consequences tomorrow or that we will get a task done "sometime," then we should think of this as choosing to accept the consequences of that behavior. If we always frame procrastination in that way—as a choice we are making to accept the results of not completing a certain project or process—then we may be able to motivate ourselves into making a different decision. Yes, the unforeseen occurs and sometimes we all miss a self-imposed deadline. But then our most immediate ownership responsibility is to readjust our schedule to accommodate that slippage.

But just as common and with consequences far beyond the individual is the way that agreements between colleagues and between professors and students are often treated irresponsibly. A wholesale disregard of agreed-upon deadlines is strangely endemic to our profession. Academics regularly complete projects or send in material weeks, months, even years after they promised it, without any discussion or even an apology. They regularly fail to return graded papers to students when promised; indeed, they sometimes *never* return them. I have even known academics who habitually neglect to write letters of recommendation for students and seriously jeopardize those students' chances at graduate school or jobs because of that irresponsibility. One might term such behavior "unprofessional," except for the fact that it is so common that in some ways it is actually normal "professional" behavior. But certainly such irresponsibility tears at the fabric of our community; it is a form of dishonesty and disrespect for our students and each other. I cannot know what the consequences will be for you if I miss a deadline that we have set together. It may jeopardize your tenure and promotion; it may ruin your vacation; it may make your daily life hellish. I can ask you for that information, and we can negotiate a different deadline if my schedule must be changed. But too often we fail even to engage in that exchange of information because, of course, admitting that we will miss a deadline is an admission of our own fallibility, and that is, unfortunately, wholly incompatible with some academics' sense of their own masterful selfhood. A lot of energy has to go into protecting such a ridiculous construction.

On the other hand, if we do complete projects on schedule, and to the best of our abilities, and are proactive in the ways that we interact with those who are depending upon us, we can actively create a better community. That in and of itself is a laudable and energizing goal to set for ourselves, one that we can accomplish and reaccomplish every day.

5. Deal with and appropriately respond to failures or setbacks.

All of the above sounds very mechanical, neat, and "controlled," but obviously and inevitably, setbacks occur. Even beyond unexpected impingements on our time, which may be accommodated in a revised schedule, we may receive a rejection, be rebuffed in our application or request, or read an unfavorable review of our research or teaching. If we have tied our entire sense of accomplishment and selfhood to someone else's approval or a narrowly defined product or outcome, then such an occurrence can wreak havoc on our personal and professional lives.

But that does not have to be the case. If we invest ourselves partly— or even largely—in the process of continuous learning and professional reinvention, then the receipt of bad news becomes a part of the *process* of discussion and response. We can always learn from a review of our teaching or research, and even from a rejection or a "failed" application. Perhaps we receive information that is vital to the project concerned or are given the opportunity to learn something about ourselves and our own reactions and processing of information. But we can decide how to respond to or use undesired information or unforeseen setbacks. If we view our professional selves as organic and responsive, then no single disappointment or even string of disappointments will threaten that selfhood. Deciding to construct a professional selfhood on principles of growth, change, and dialogue gives us a way of processing all informa- tion that we receive. While we will probably never welcome criticism or negative responses, we can see them as part of long and productive processes.

6. We should allow our goals to change thoughtfully as our context changes, as new information comes our way, and as new opportunities open up.

Nothing that I have said above is meant to promote static or otherwise lifeless commitments to fixed goals or senses of selfhood. While irresponsibility and constantly shifting goals and desires are forms of self-destructive behavior, all our goals and selves change over time. They should change thoughtfully and responsibly, with reference both to institutional expectations and needs, our commitments to others, and an honest appraisal of the consequences of change. But nevertheless change they should and must. As we enter new jobs, encounter and learn from colleagues, and discover new fields of interest, our priorities and plans should accommodate the excitement of our discoveries. That vitality should be the core of our professional lives; it makes us exciting teachers, innovative scholars, and energetic department members. We should never forget that we are engaged in creating and recreating our selfhoods on a daily basis.

A Practical Example

Broad talking points are all well and good, but I also want to offer a brief example of what I've been discussing. No project posed more challenges to me in terms of scheduling and goal definition than the book at hand. Because of other writing commitments, I knew I only had about a year to complete *The Academic Self*. I knew when I could begin my actual writing on it and by when I needed to have a manuscript ready to send to press. I spent two weeks doing preliminary planning, making decisions on how the chapters would be organized, scheduling broadly every week of work for the next year, and scheduling precisely every day of work for the next month. As indicated above, I drew carefully on my knowledge of my previous writing and revision speeds. My schedule shifted by a few weeks (in dialogue with my press editor) and certainly the organization and contents of the book changed dramatically as I actually wrote it, but my commitment to processing it with care and ongoing attentiveness never wavered. When helpful readers' reports arrived, I returned to my calendar and scheduled accordingly again.

I use both calendars and dry-erase boards—three of the latter, in fact—to make vivid and clear outlines and schedules, ones that are easily altered or augmented as necessary. For the purposes of this project, I wrote out on my wall calendar what I needed to have accomplished by the end of each month I devoted to this book in order to have a complete manuscript by the deadline. On the first of my dry-erase boards, I recorded certain overarching ideas that I wanted to make sure I remembered as I did all my work on the project. On another, unit/chapter deadlines and all other impending deadlines (pedagogical, institutional, personal, etc.) were recorded so that I did not jeopardize any of the many commitments that I have. On the last, I created a working outline of my plan for the chapter or unit on which I was writing (and using a dry-erase board meant that I could work with it—rethink, change, and augment it—easily). Finally, I always carry that day book in which I scheduled my work and writing hour by hour for the next month or more. If something unexpected happened or I decided to take a day off, I worked with the calendar to reshuffle or add the bit of extra work necessary to succeeding days to remain on schedule. But the important thing was and is to always see the precise consequences of making a decision to take on a new responsibility or take a break. We often deceive ourselves when we think we can make up time "somehow"; we regularly miss our deadlines because we ignore the implications of our daily, even hourly, work habits.

∾

In thus "owning" our work habits in the ways I suggest above, we are actually much better equipped to avoid what is commonly called "burnout." What do we mean by burnout and what steps in the process of becoming burned out are noticeable and potentially avoidable?

Limited professional activity is not the defining characteristic of burnout; it could indicate a thoughtful redirection of priorities toward one's personal life. As the result of a series of carefully considered decisions and a process of critical reflection, such self-aware, self-reflexive activity is not what I wish to focus on here, since it already indicates ownership. By "burnout" I mean, instead, a state *not* clearly chosen or desired, one of frustration or involving a sense of defeat that persists for

long periods of time, if not the remainder of a career. Al Gini in *My Job,*
My Self points to three common components of burnout in the corporate
world: "emotional exhaustion," "depersonalization," and "reduced personal achievement" (131). All of these can manifest themselves in the
academic world too. They are often evidenced in angry or sneering interactions with colleagues and students, and in a cynical dismissal of others'
goals and achievements. These aspects of individual burnout can poison,
in clear and dramatic fashion, a teaching environment or an entire academic community.

But burnout is not always so dramatic or interpersonally displayed;
indeed, for academics, isolation is perhaps burnout's most telling component—isolation from the flow of conversation in a field of interest, from
intellectually and professionally active colleagues, and from the changing
needs of students. As I suggested earlier, such isolation—especially as it
leads almost inevitably to an anachronistic base of knowledge—is a particularly grave disservice to students. Our burnout is not just our own concern; a continuing attachment to a larger context of scholarship and
intellectual exchange is fundamental to the work we do at teaching
schools, at liberal arts colleges, and at research universities.

If we frame "burnout" in that way—as a failure to meet our pedagogical and communal responsibilities—then its avoidance or remediation
becomes one of the clear imperatives of our professional lives. Some of
what I will say in the coming pages will appear obvious or even banal to
some readers; if so, then you are probably not in that process of burning
out. But read and think about these microsteps carefully, because someone—your office mate, cherished colleague, or best friend—might now or
in the future need your help and gentle mentoring. Burnout is avoidable
and even reversible through patient attention to professional self-identity and to planning. Supple senses of professional self-identity and a continuing attachment to career planning and goal setting mean that even
the most trying situations and unsettling setbacks—ones leading potentially to burnout—can be approached as intellectual and professional
challenges, ones that invite our reinterpretation and the retextualization
of our own professional schedules, goals, and priorities. Indeed, this
always depends upon the ownership choices that I point to in previous
chapters; we must decide to engage with our own careers as textual enti-
ties, ones that are as complex and intriguing as any novel, poem, or institutional setting.

But what if the sum total of the personal decisions and external forces encountered in one's career has led one already to a state of isolation, inertia, or paralysis? First, it might be useful to re-term this a "stalled" period that simply precedes a regaining of intellectual movement and professional energy. The remedy for such stalls is actually the same as its prevention, to which I will turn below. But the process of challenging and changing any professional self-identity that is entrenched is certainly difficult, especially if that self-identity is one of inertia. Successfully challenging that inertia depends upon small steps and concrete action today, tomorrow, and the day after. It may depend upon placing oneself mentally back in the state one occupied as a graduate student, studying intensely and reacquainting oneself thoroughly with the flow of conversation in a changed and changing area of professional interest. That is difficult to do, obviously. It requires that we continue to teach our classes or perform our other duties and at the same time devote ourselves to intense scholarly inquiry, just as graduate students do who work a full-time job and still pursue their studies. Stalled faculty members can do it too, if they make the choice to place themselves mentally and humbly in that state of apprenticeship.

But any such process—one of reconnection and professional reinvigoration—depends upon deciding what component part of that process will be accomplished without further delay. Below, I discuss some very small steps in professional involvement and invigoration, focusing on how to engage in scholarly and professional work beyond our local contexts in steady ways. If we are mentoring others in this process, frustration and impatience are of little use. No one can begin to publish again after years away from the flow of conversation without first completing some very basic tasks: rejoining organizations, reading and listening carefully. But a mentor's work can only go so far. However forcefully you may tell me what I "need to do," only I can decide which one of the following I must and will do by 5 p.m. today.

Ten Small Steps in the Process of Professional Invigoration (or in remedying isolation and burnout)

1. Join and remain a member of your national professional organization or of organizations devoted to your specific area of interest and expertise.

I know this will seem obvious to many readers, but if you name to yourself the angriest and most isolated academics among your acquaintances, they are probably the ones who no longer interest themselves in the intellectual community represented and fostered by professional organizations. As a step in maintaining or renewing professional connection, it is as easy as visiting a website or writing a check. Beyond simple membership comes the responsibility of participation: reading the professional journals, attending the conferences, listening to and engaging in professional conversations. All of those take time—time that must be found and scheduled—but it is time invested in our own professional self-identities and in the base of knowledge upon which we draw for the benefit of students. Simply attending conferences, listening to and thinking over the work of others is perhaps the simplest step to commit to and build upon if we are currently disconnected or stalled.

2. Continue to read widely in your area of interest (or reconnect by beginning to read widely again).

Graduate students reading this book may say "well, duh, of course," but they would be surprised to discover how rarely some academics read new critical work. If our continuing sense of connection and intellectual involvement depends upon our awareness of the flow of conversation in our fields, some of that engagement may come from our attentive listening at conferences, but most of it will necessarily take the form of regular reading of newly published material. Even when we are pressed with teaching or administrative duties, it is vital that the daily and weekly reading plans that many of us established by necessity in graduate school—just to prepare for examinations or the writing of our dissertations—continue to be a part of our professional self-identities. To stop reading journals, new books, and about new theories and methodologies is to begin to atrophy.

Every day we can add to the knowledge base that we have to draw upon in our own writing and to pass along to students in our classes. We may only have thirty minutes to devote to new reading in the morning or evening, but that investment of time in our continuing competence in our fields should be considered a professional obligation, not an option or luxury. Indeed, a self-imposed assignment of daily reading is no more than what we ask of our students. That integration of our requirements of others and of ourselves is key to the owning and making textually whole our professional self-identities.

3. Define off-campus career goals precisely and carefully.

Precise and thoughtful goal definition is key to maintaining a sense of accomplishment and contentment. Only by knowing exactly what it is we would like to achieve in and through our work can we begin to make effective use of the other planning and scheduling tips that I mentioned earlier. In graduate school, this was relatively easy because we were preparing to take a scheduled examination or we were struggling to finish our dissertation by a certain date. This will change dramatically in our careers after graduate school; our goals are often substantially self-generated and can take many different forms and directions. Sometimes institutions are very explicit about their requirements for continuing employment—a book by a certain tenure decision date, for example—but teaching schools in particular are far less directive. Even those institutions that do make explicit demands depend upon the individual academic to make and hold to intermediate goals and deadlines with little intervention other than annual reviews. This amorphousness, which hits many academics most intensely *after* tenure or after the completion of a book or major project, can be energizing, stressful, and/or potentially paralyzing.

First, as indicated earlier, we cannot tie our sense of accomplishment solely to a specific, immediate response to our work. Therefore even as we articulate professional goals carefully, we should remember to invest with the greatest worth the involvement with and completion of a particular project, rather than its immediate reception. We might set as a goal the submission of an article to a journal after a six-month period of writing, but not set as our explicit goal its acceptance, which we cannot count on. This may seem like semantic play, but I am actually talking about a very serious attitudinal difference. If we demand a specific response to our work, then we are setting ourselves up for bitterness and burnout if that response is not forthcoming. We have to get more out of our work than simply the unqualified approval of peer reviewers or editorial boards.

For example, we might set as our concrete goal the completion and submission to a press of a book-length project in three years. Of course, even that simple act of submission is a form of "making public" our work, and it represents an entrée into conversation with the larger professional world. It is not a "publication," but it can serve as an appropriate and precise goal, for it is one that is substantially within our power to achieve. We might then set as our next goal the careful revision of our manuscript as readers' reports come in, though the success of that process, too, should not depend narrowly upon a certain subsequent response by the same press to our work. It might instead involve the completion of our work toward the goal of resubmitting the revised manuscript to the same or perhaps a different press.

No one should set our goals for us (though certainly they should be set in response to institutional requirements), so I hesitate to comment upon the wisdom of any specific goal here. But certainly any goal involving individual fame at the expense of communal responsibilities and the work we do with colleagues and students dismays me. Some of the most miserable people that I have ever known—alcoholic, angry, and insecure—have been very "famous" in their fields. Any career plan that centers largely on autonomous achievement will probably lead to the paranoia that Cathy Davidson mentioned earlier in this book. No vita, however impressive, is worth the personal and communal misery that comes with such a narrow life.

4. Set and maintain a daily writing schedule, however modest.

This is a simple suggestion to make and, of course, a harder one to keep. But I maintain my involvement in professional conversations in my fields of interest by making sure that no work day goes by without writing something. Even if I only manage to write for a half hour in the morning or late afternoon, or set as my goal the generation of a paragraph, such work builds up steadily toward the completion of a project. Just as the success of savings plans depend upon steady, even if modest, contributions, so, too, does the success of a writing plan depend upon regular and unfailing incremental progress. I take every Sunday off, but no other day goes by without some form of writing, revision, or other work toward goal completion. While some readers may have to adjust this scheduling tip to reflect their own goals and time constraints—perhaps setting a weekly rather than daily schedule—remember that if you are working to change an entrenched pattern of behavior (procrastination, let us say), it is vital focus on small, regular units of progress toward a larger objective. The *daily* achievement of micro-goals here is key.

You can do the math. If you simply write *one page per day*, you will have the rough draft of a book manuscript in a year.

5. Present conference papers, as they help you meet your goals.

As indicated above, remaining professionally invigorated or reinvigorating oneself depends upon the quality and quantity of one's engagement in conversations in one's area of interest. That engagement is often realized and deepened at academic conferences, where we offer our interpretations and professional opinions as formal presentations, as responses to others' presentations, over dinners and coffee, and by way of connecting and reconnecting with colleagues from across the region or nation. Some of the most useful feedback I have ever received on my work has been given in open discussion at conferences after I delivered a paper. Rather than dreading a difficult question or a skeptical response, I hope to hear objections or requests for clarification from the audience, since surely many of the same or much more profound reservations will come from readers of my written work.

But as energizing and useful as the process of conference presentations are, they are also time-consuming. They are one important component of participation in scholarly conversations but are usually valued as an early step toward making one's ideas and analyses more widely available and rigorously scrutinized through actual publication. Indeed, frequent conference participation can be an avoidance technique, if presentations are not clearly part of a process of deepening one's research and completing initiated projects. Depending upon how one's institution values a conference presentation as research, one may even wish to stop presenting papers, especially in areas of new interest, until ongoing projects are completed (perhaps sent out for publication consideration). We should use conference presentations as they help us realize our goals beyond the conference itself.

6. Invest time and energy in brief writing projects, also as they help you meet your goals.

As we are conducting research and deepening our knowledge base, we are usually reading widely. As we encounter newly published research in our areas of interest, it is often very useful to write our responses to that research and publish them in the form of book reviews. Such reviews allow us to think through our ideas, syntheses, and disagreements carefully, often with the help of a book review editor, and thereby add to the conversation in our fields. The same can be true for encyclopedia-type entries and other contracted work. If they fall within our established or burgeoning areas of research commitment, they provide important occasions for bringing together our reading and our insights into articulations that add to the ongoing exchange of ideas. Indeed, even when constrained by narrow formats and formulae of presentation, writers can use these opportunities to advance an original argument and advance the process of deepening their knowledge base as they prepare related projects, perhaps an article or even a book. Depending upon how an institution values the publication of reviews and contracted essays, such writing may or may not be appropriate ends in themselves.

But if an institution does not value them as significant forms of publication—and especially if one is in the tenure and promotion process—they should only form part of an overall research strategy in which they abet, rather than delay, the completion of projects that will earn the desired institutional recognition. I was told early in my career to avoid writing too many book reviews, because "it looks bad." In other words, it looks like I cannot or will not publish work that is longer, that draws on more original research, and that is refereed. I have largely ignored that advice because reviews are always part of other, ongoing research, and they are regarded as legitimate publications by my home institution. But certainly I have said no to many writing projects—reviews or contracted essays—that do not dovetail with and support my other research. Here, as always, it is important to have a well-thought-out set of short-, medium-, and long-term goals that allows one to judge the wisdom of participating in any project that draws upon one's time and energy. Consider all offers or possible projects vis-à-vis the professional statement described in chapter 1. For example, a book review might take several weeks of work. It is important to consider and clarify to oneself precisely why one is devoting that much time to a short-term project that may or may not be valued highly by one's institution.

7. Understand the process and timeline of manuscript review and publication.

In completing an article or a book-length manuscript, and considering its submission to a journal or press, it is important to know what the process involves (how many readers, whether they are simultaneously consulted or sequentially consulted), how long a given publication venue takes to make a decision, and then how long it takes them to publish accepted work. The Modern Language Association publishes guides to journals and presses that often include such information. I pay particular attention to these guidelines because I don't want requests for revision, for example, to come in unexpectedly and disrupt my progress on other projects, to which I may be committed in a very narrowly time-bound fashion. It is especially important to research and reflect on such external processes if a decision or actual publication is needed as part of a tenure and/or promotion process. If it typically takes a press six months to a year to make a firm publication decision on a book manuscript and if you need a firm contract for tenure, then you are certainly courting disaster if you do not schedule carefully to leave that full year for a decision. Even if you do leave the full year, it is always possible that the decision will be no. It would be far more responsible to build into any narrowly time-bound process—a five-year plan for book production before a tenure decision, for example—enough time to revise and resubmit or go through the process at a second press. That is why long-term scheduling is absolutely key to "owning" one's professional self-identity. You cannot control the outcome of processes such as review and publication decisions—you may receive obtuse readers' reports or meet with duplicity at a particular press or journal—but you can maximize your chances of receiving a positive decision by a date that you know about years in advance. Your own process *and* the process at a press or journal are both parts of a larger process of review and decision making if you are pre-tenure or are being considered for promotion to full professor at a specific time.

8. Establish positive working relationships with presses and journals.

Editors and editorial boards at journals and presses encounter all the attitudes and work habits—positive and negative, responsible and irresponsible—that I have been discussing in this book. They find some authors unreliable and arrogant and others highly responsible and affable. While the quality of the author's work will play a key role in whether or not it is published, the text of an article or book manuscript is not the only text to which the press or journal will be responding. If they find that the text of the academic's own professional self-identity—in the form of irresponsible or "diva"-like behavior—is one with which they cannot engage productively, then the unacceptable nature of that text may override the positives of the print text.

The benefits of working responsibly with a press or journal—returning e-mails promptly, fulfilling commitments on deadline, engaging in dialogue rather than monologue on revisions and marketing—extend beyond the publication of the immediate manuscript. Positive working relationships with editors and editorial boards are the basis for future projects planned jointly—advance contracts on books, guest editing assignments at journals, etc.—and for appointments to editorial boards and as readers. It is best to approach the process of manuscript placement as itself part of a much longer and more complex process of professional reputation building that involves responsible behavior and productive partnerships with editors.

But it is also true that editors and editorial boards may be plagued by the same behavioral problems mentioned above. If you cannot trust your editor, if he/she fails to meet deadlines or engage in dialogue, then you must decide whether or not this individual is someone whom you wish to trust with an important aspect of your career—perhaps tenure and promotion. Research your press or editor; ask other professionals about his/her reputation and work habits. See the processes and personalities of the press or journal with whom you may be working as part of the text of your own professional life. Approach that text critically and carefully.

9. *Withdraw gracefully and responsibly from unproductive professional relationships.*

The same is true for all relationships that have profound career consequences. Collaborative projects can be highly rewarding or they can be nightmarish. Similarly, if you are a guest editor or a book review editor, you may find that you quickly receive evidence that a certain academic cannot be trusted to fulfill obligations. Obviously, many unexpected occurrences can lead to deadlines slipping or work being postponed. I am not talking here about such minor delays or inevitable adjustments. Rather, I am suggesting that we pay close attention to the textuality of each other's work habits, and if we receive evidence of a pattern or recurring narrative of irresponsible behavior or sloppy work, then we should consider withdrawing gracefully from a particular professional relationship. Perhaps the most positive way of stating this is that we should always value highly and express gratitude often to those professionals who treat their colleagues with respect and see their professional promises and obligations as the base matter of our common academic life.

10. Establish micro-support networks that both nurture and challenge you professionally.

In valuing and nurturing those ties, in seeing our professional interactions as perhaps the most important part of our professional life, we can establish a support system or network of micro-systems that enrich us in many ways. While I will focus directly on collegiality in my next chapter, I do want to emphasize here that we must see our processes—of research, of curricular redesign, of pedagogical innovation—as constituent parts of larger group processes. Functionality as well as dysfunctionality can be collectively reinforced. A support system of departmental colleagues, of like-minded professionals on e-mail lists, of friends at conferences and nearby institutions, can help us weather the inevitable stresses of professional life, but they should also challenge us: to continue to learn and expand intellectually and to remain vibrant members of our profession. Our support systems should spur us to activity rather than abet stasis or inactivity. Again, we should value highly those colleagues who help us overcome obstacles and who also enliven our collective professional existences.

∼

If we schedule carefully, prioritize responsibly, and work steadily toward the completion of professional goals, our personal lives, recreation and vacation time, and interpersonal relationships are all protected. As Matthias Schubnell relates in his contribution to the SCMLA panel that I have mentioned several times, his own time- and career-management strategies were perfected because he "increasingly felt torn between the demands of scholarship in conjunction with [his] teaching duties and the desire to spend as much time as possible with [his] two small children who deserved and greatly appreciated [his] attention" (3). I know far too many people who work through the evening, who neglect friends, children, and partners, who are stressed out and miserable. And invariably, these are the individuals who are *least* engaged with their own processes and work habits, who react in ad hoc fashion, who procrastinate and remain professionally unfocused. But I have also met, know, and know of many happy and very active professionals about whose own sources of vitality I would love to hear much more. As I have said all along, the texts of our own professional lives are ones that we must share widely. They are scripts that we can mull over, critically examine, and adapt for our own purposes as we engage in our individual and collective professional "performances." I offer my script here and can only hope that others will respond with alternatives and generous, frank articulations.

chapter four

Collegiality, Community and Change

i N THIS FINAL CHAPTER, I want to turn to an aspect of our professional lives and self-identities that is often wholly ignored, a text that is not yet part of the emerging canon of widely discussed professional studies texts: collegiality. In graduate school and in professional studies workshops we are trained in the nuts and bolts of academic career skills and career building: research and publication, pedagogy and effective teaching, marketing ourselves and packaging our accomplishments. A spate of recent books, including Emily Toth's Ms. *Mentor's Impeccable Advice for Women in Academia* and *The Chicago Guide to Your Academic Career* (Goldsmith et al.), summarizes this information usefully for general reference purposes. But rarely, if ever, do we discuss our professional lives in their communal aspects, the ways that we operate always as members of committees, departments, universities, professional organizations, and an even more diffuse social web of scholars and teaching intellectuals with sometimes overlapping and sometimes widely divergent interests, goals, and priorities. Tellingly, the aforementioned *Chicago Guide* discusses collegiality only as the necessity of "getting along with colleagues" (142–46), not as something that is in fact central to our lives and careers. Indeed, collegiality is often considered as simply another job "burden."

As quoted earlier, Deborah Tannen speaks perceptively in *The Argument Culture* about how certain pernicious modes of thinking are ubiquitous and self-replicating: "the assumption that challenge and attack are the best modes of scholarly inquiry is pervasive in American scholarly communities. . . . Many graduate programs are geared to training young scholars in rigorous thinking, defined as the ability to launch and field verbal attacks" (266). She calls this "the argument culture of academia—our conception of intellectual exchange as a metaphorical battle" (267). In a follow-up essay, Tannen elaborates on this point: "The way we train our students frequently reflects the battle metaphor. . . . We assign scholarly work for them to read, then invite them to tear it apart. That is helpful to an extent, but it often means that they don't learn to do the harder work of integrating ideas, or of considering the work's historical or disciplinary context. Moreover, it fosters in students a stance of arrogance and narrow-mindedness" ("Agonism" B7). Certainly social skills are at best tangential to our professional training programs. We can occasionally pick up the concrete behaviors and broader attitudes abetting collegiality by participating as graduate students in committee work, in collaborative projects, in dissertation support groups, and by simply bonding and strategizing with our peers. However, rarely, if ever, is such socialization recognized as vital to our professional success, vitality, and equilibrium. Indeed, such socialization is often more than offset by the many professional forces working in a very different direction, that is, toward a valuation of competitive struggle, individualistic achievement, monologic presentation, monographic publication, critical "distinction," and a professorial identity constructed around principles of autonomy and mastery. "Success" is almost always individually defined, as we compete for awards, recognition, and, of course, scarce jobs. Yet when we actually begin our jobs, much of our happiness and sense of fulfillment will come from whether or not we are members of a healthy community, one that we must contribute to supplely, responsibly, at times even humbly. The shift is difficult. That it is ever achieved seems miraculous.

Furthermore, many other forces besides our own naturalized drive toward professional distinction and fierce competition work against collegiality. As Bill Readings explores in *The University in Ruins,* and as I have discussed throughout this book, we are at a moment of profound dissensus in our academic work. In English and cultural studies departments, we no longer agree necessarily or fundamentally on our methodologies, goals, or our base-level definitions of what an academic is or does. A very wide variety of opinions will almost inevitably exist within any given department, and not only about pedagogical, curricular, and research priorities, but even about what does or does not constitute a *legitimate* subject for research or teaching. Only those institutions that attempt to enforce dogma as their central identity base—strict religious institutions, for example—can escape somewhat from the fragmentation of the larger profession. For the rest of us, dissensus is here to stay because of the proliferation of our own politicized self-definitions, our increasingly diverse student populations, and the very self-reflexivity that this book identifies as socially pervasive and that it works to foster. Any attempt to impose homogeneity on such a heterogenous population will simply end in frustration and abject dysfunction.

So what should be our communal ideal, given this inescapable epistemological heterogeneity? It must be an intellectually energizing, functional coexistence, one in which, as J. Hillis Miller has suggested, "people with very different opinions are able to dwell amicably together and respect each other's opinions" (228). He sketches the outline of what a functional dissensual department might look like:

> [I]t is a model that is very difficult to embody and institutionalize . . . because the tradition that I and most of us in the profession were brought up on says that if you talk long enough, eventually you will come to consensus—it is the Habermasian model. Consensus rarely occurs, however, without doing violence to some of the positions that people started out with. I don't see why consensus should necessarily be the goal. What I favor instead is a Lyotardian model, rather than a Habermasian one, a community of dissensus. This model recognizes that groups must have cooperation with each other within an institutional setting, but that they may have critical methods and goals that are fundamentally incompatible with each other. All of these . . . could reside amicably within the same department, if each is courteous and respectful of those people who hold positions with which he or she disagrees. That does not mean that forceful argument should not occur, but that this disagreement need not have consensus as its horizon. (228–29)

The ties that bind us together during those periods of disagreement and manifestations of profound epistemological disjunction must be ones of personal, collegial investment. Indeed, these ties can only be the result of *decisions* to commit to and identify with the department or other group even in its dissensual state. And in these personal decisions and in the numerous ways they are enacted daily, community building, community nurturance, and community maintenance are the responsibility of every member of a department. But just because someone else is reneging on his or her responsibility does not let you off of the hook of your responsibility. As with other chapters, this one will focus on our individual fulfillment of such responsibilities, whatever others do or fail to do. This micro-"self" in "self-help" is always the necessary building block for a well-functioning community.

To provide a broad frame for our discussion of that communal life, first it is important to recognize that all communities have both synchronic and diachronic aspects. At a given moment, we can isolate their structures, productive patterns of behavior, and the roles that individuals play within them. That type of analysis of the text of a department (the community on which I will focus most often here) is necessary background to considering and committing oneself to projects and processes of change discussed later in this chapter. But recognizing the inevitability of and potential inherent in those processes over time—a diachronic perspective—is also necessary. However functional or dysfunctional they are at a given moment, communities will always change, and that change can be for the better or for the worse. Indeed, committing oneself to maintaining an evolving positive environment is just as important as committing oneself to improving a dysfunctional one.

And this is how "self"-help takes us beyond the atomized "self." So often derided as solipsistic, "self-help" can point toward a community helping itself—through processes of planning, collective goal setting, and problem solving—even as individuals often must take the lead in initiating such processes. Simply put, it is "both/and," not "either/or." Thus as much as this book values and promotes professional goal setting and achievement, it does so with a direct challenge to the academy: to see always individual achievement as part of a web of support, intellectual nurturance, and communal goal setting. This is not to say that communities of professionals are warm and cozy spaces in which all disagreements are nervously avoided (and, thereby, even the most dysfunctional behaviors passively abetted). From the outset, dissensus renders that unlikely, if not impossible. But rancor, in particular, is not inevitable.

Yet that shift from atomized professional to responsible community member is difficult to achieve, and in fact, it is even difficult to illustrate or describe with accuracy and precision. But first and foremost, realizing collegiality demands a deliberate commitment of identity on the part of the individual academic. A job candidate whom my department's hiring committee once interviewed (but whom another lucky department ended up hiring) made during his interview an insightful observation about the destructive ethos of "free agency" that seems to pervade the academy today—the mindset that institutional affiliations are always only temporary and that individuals owe little to their departments or institutions beyond the very short-term (perhaps as short as one academic term). Many broad social forces account for such attitudes and certainly numerous microcosmic professional forces exacerbate them: the rise in the use of adjunct labor, the demand by some institutions for "stellar" professional profiles, and the eager raiding of departments for such "stars." But the result of such a mindset of migrancy are communities of disconnected, often jealous and highly competitive individuals, whose communal bond and social skill level is meager or nonexistent.

That understanding of our often very weak social tie is my starting point here. I will subdivide the following discussion into two sections that address first base-level communal responsibilities and attitudes ("Citizenship 101," you might say) and then the processes and payoffs of communal change. I offer no panacea but do maintain my optimism that as individuals rigorously trained in critical thinking skills, we can turn, finally, those skills to the text of our own communal behavior and sense of collegial selves. Whether superbly functional, abjectly dysfunctional, or (usually) somewhere in between, our departments and our home institutions demand and deserve such engagement. Indeed, even as we cultural critics so often and eagerly engage the functions and dysfunctions of national and international culture, let us remember always *to put and keep our own house in order.*

Talking Points on Professorial Attitudes and Identities

1. Our careers are largely local, even if they have national aspects or implications.

In stating this, I am asking that we reframe our conception of what a "career" means. The quality and intellectual excitement of our daily professional lives may be strongly affected by the flow of national discussions in our fields and enhanced dramatically by positive responses to our work in a wide variety of professional venues. However, our interactions with our classes, our colleagues, and our chairs, deans, and provosts will largely determine (or will have already determined) whether or not we are employed in this profession six years after first entering it. Indeed, our immediate institutional environment accounts for just how bearable we will find every day as we awake and face its challenges. We should never forget in any self-motivated quest for scholarly recognition that we live— and will be judged locally on our behavior—as citizens in the microcommunities of our departments and universities.

Indeed, as thoroughly as we are trained in graduate school to be autonomous beings—solitary scholars and masterful teachers—much of our work is quite the opposite: highly social. Both our scholarship and teaching are at their best when conducted in energetic conversation with others, but just as importantly, our interactions with colleagues—our willingness to share the responsibilities of service, our contributions to networks of response and support for others' work, our constructive or destructive behaviors and attitudes in meetings and hallway interactions—are ongoing parts of our professional performances. They are the day-to-day matter of what we do as academics and are an aspect of the "text" of our professional existence that deserves as much critical scrutiny as any other.

And certainly the local rewards for being a good citizen—as well as for teaching effectively and succeeding in scholarly pursuits—can be tangible: pay raises, promotion (early or on schedule), and the esteem of students, colleagues, and administrators. But far more importantly, our contributions to a healthy collegial environment repay us daily in the nurturance, support, and sharing of work that make our own lives easier and more productive.

2. Our current job may be our only or our last job.

Some people are told (as I was) to work as hard as you can to "write yourself out of" your first job if it is at a teaching school (or other institution judged inferior by common professional standards). However, that is not the most productive or the healthiest attitude to bring to any affiliation. Of course options may one day present themselves for moving to a different university or type of institution, to a different city or region of the country. If our goals include an active research agenda and our work is noticed, we may have many complex choices to make over the course of our careers.

But we cannot and should not count on it. Given the current and continuing job crunch—the high number of applicants for almost every position advertised—we must recognize the likelihood that our home institutions at this moment will be our homes for our entire careers, and to act accordingly. Making that mental shift, identifying with our students, colleagues, and support staff, and seeing ourselves as part of our department's and university's future allows us to prioritize appropriately and to begin to judge how we can improve that local context or help maintain its best qualities. As I discuss below, processes of local change—curricular, programmatic, and certainly morale-based—may take many years of steady work to accomplish; only by seeing ourselves as sharing in the rewards of such processes can we maintain the level of commitment we will need to do such work on a daily, weekly, or monthly basis. We may have a very tough decision to make if we are offered a chance to move during such a process—especially when we know that our work is key to the success of it—but such a *possibility* should never outweigh the *likelihood* that we will remain a part of that local community.

3. The "success" and happiness of our local careers depends often upon (at least) three things: first, and certainly, our thorough understanding and careful meeting of institutional expectations.

Indeed, whether or not we are even allowed to be part of that future is dependent upon our being committed enough to our institutions to acquaint ourselves with its expectations, its decision-making processes, and its priorities and needs. Those who focus simply on their careers beyond their campus are courting disaster. Thus, as I have emphasized throughout this book, it is important always to treat our local contexts as texts. Its most obviously textual aspects are its published rules governing behavior, promotion, tenure, and decision making. Those are texts with which we should acquaint ourselves immediately and thoroughly. Understanding thoroughly how decisions are made means reading carefully the chain of command in our institutions: its system of committees with their specific charges, the roles of chairs, deans, provosts, presidents, and chancellors. It also involves asking about and observing carefully the ways decisions are made and how they are respected or not by others in the system. As I expand upon this discussion below, I am not suggesting that you ever become Machiavellian—sneaky political games almost always backfire and result in disaster—but I am strongly urging that we all need to be observant and understand who has ability to affect our jobs and job security, and also help us effect any changes that we may decide to promote.

4. Second, local "success" and happiness depends upon our behaviors, attitudes, and interactions within the communities of our departments, colleges, and universities.

This takes us to the heart of what it means to be a "good" colleague: the degree of responsibility, reliability, and thoughtfulness of our day-to-day actions and interactions. Simply put, we cannot be good colleagues if we are convinced that we are infallible, that our perspectives are singularly "truthful," that our inevitably partial and tendentious answers to complex questions are the only ones legitimate, or that we have little or nothing to learn from others. This explains, of course, why academic departments, especially those made up of individuals trained to be skilled "critics," can be particularly volatile places. Graduate school teaches us to argue very effectively for the singular legitimacy of our readings and responses to complex and even unanswerable questions. Of course, a few individuals may even gravitate toward this profession because that validation of "monism" (Wayne Booth's terminology from *Critical Understanding*) meets a preexisting desire to find a way to "prove" themselves to be possessed of superior knowledge or understanding, and to find validation for a hubris that is already part of their self-identities. I am convinced, however, that most aspiring academics come to graduate school with far more supple perspectives and senses of self but are asked there to adopt a narrowly, oppositionally defined "critic"'s identity in order to survive and thrive.

I would hope that we would all admit that *none of us is solely and always right*. But putting our awareness of that fact into daily practice is indeed a challenge. In order to be a good colleague, we have to admit and remember our own limitations. Furthermore, we also have to forgive ourselves for them, for not meeting some impossible ideal of perfect professorial mastery. If we are carrying around a burden of denial or unadmitted or unresolved self-castigation, it is easy for us to lash out in anger at the imperfections of others. Arrogance and insecurity go hand in hand, each feeding the other, and both inevitably wreaking havoc on our interpersonal relationships. While this brief book cannot address personal self-esteem issues, certainly any of us with continuing and profound problems with our self-images and in our behavior patterns should use the intelligence we possess to seek out appropriate help.

But being part of a community means that we also have to learn to respond appropriately to the inevitable mistakes that others will make. Sometimes those mistakes are very small—forgetting to return a book or to attend a meeting; sometimes they are larger and could jeopardize important projects and processes. We should not forget the behavior of others when making decisions about the future, but we must also find ways of continuing to coexist with fallible colleagues with whom we may be working for years or decades to come. Corrupt behavior and intentional cruelty are especially worth remembering and responding to appropriately; I am *not* suggesting that we allow ourselves or others to be victimized. But within departments and other groups of academics the most shocking and destructive reactions often occur over very minor lapses, failures, and small differences of opinion. I have seen colleagues explode over imagined slights to cherished authors. I have seen others fume over the small personality quirks—the facial mannerisms or voice patterns—of their colleagues. Dysfunction often begins with unnecessarily harsh judgements and lingering, silly grudges. And fully owning up to this fact also means acknowledging that to linger in anger or in grievance is to *decide* to do continuing damage to our communities.

Beyond offering forgiveness for past mistakes, we must also recognize that those communities are made up of individuals with continuing and future needs that are as legitimate as our own. The primary way that we are taught to value ourselves in capitalistic society is through our success at acquisition. Our worth, we are told, is somehow measurable through our salaries and other material aspects of our personal and professional lives. Of course, by deciding to enter the academy, we are foregoing some of the most extreme forms of material reward that we might find in the business world. Yet even after deciding to enter a modestly paying profession, some very destructive and pernicious comparison-based dynamics in constructing and maintaining our self-identities can still linger and jeopardize our communities.

If we measure our success through the articulation and meeting of our own goals, as I suggest throughout this book, we can achieve them without begrudging others their own successes. However, if we need to succeed primarily in comparison to others, then we are deciding to enter a dynamic of competition that has numerous pernicious consequences, personal and inter-personal. If I need a higher salary increase, a bigger office, or a better computer than my colleagues in order to feel like a "success," my insecurities will never be assuaged. There will always be someone whose "success" will represent a threat to my equilibrium. Comparison as the primary determinant of "success" will always threaten our relationships with colleagues and the functionality of our communities.

This is why I suggest throughout this book that we must shift our definition of professional success from one that is solely comparison-based to one emphasizing self-generated and collective goal achievement. We must shift our awareness of legitimate needs to embrace the community of our colleagues, staff, and administrators. In doing so, I can accommodate the simple, base-level fact that a colleague's "need" for the office or computer that I also "want" may be, in fact, equally or even more legitimate. Furthermore, such a shift means taking responsibility for the communal implications of our personal actions. If we demand, receive, and then misuse a grant that could have gone to another person, we have not only failed to achieve our own goals but acted in a way that has impacted others and perhaps undermined the possible achievement of their goals. To shift from a narrowly individualistic to a community-based understanding of needs and goals is not to do away with our own processes of goal setting and our responsibility for working energetically toward them, but it is to place our own agendas into a context of others' agendas, some overlapping and some inevitably (as with grants, funding, or office space) competing. It is to recognize the intricate ways our decisions, demands, and use or misuse of resources have effects beyond the autonomous self. Even if we were never trained in graduate school to think in this way, unless we can make this shift and see always the communal resonance of our individual actions and fulfillments of responsibility, then we and our communities will suffer from the myriad of antagonisms that necessarily attends competition as our operant social paradigm.

Indeed, competition and narrow, comparison-based definitions of "success" usually lead to very transient payoffs, whereas a broader community of support and validation has much more ballast and can provide continuous payoffs over long periods of time. The concrete ways that this

support is enacted involves not only reacting appropriately but also acting with the health of the community in mind, respecting others' accomplishments, and *verbalizing* that respect. If we have forgiven people for
past lapses and accepted them with their inevitable limitations, then
there is nothing lost and much to be gained from praising their achievement of their own goals. There is no common, limited store of success out
of which another individual draws at our inevitable expense: good reputation, intelligence, and even "fame" are hardly zero-sum attributes. And
even if the person whom we congratulate or praise will never return the
favor, we have contributed to a larger sense of community in a way that
should constitute a goal in and of itself. We cannot expect a collegial
department if we do not act collegially ourselves. If we accept the fact
that "community" and collegiality are positive components of our professional lives, then every decision to forego contributing to them—even in
simply neglecting to say "congratulations"—is also one for which we have
to accept responsibility.

Throughout this book I suggest that we have much to learn from each
other, and we can only realize a healthy and vibrant community if we
remind ourselves often of that fact. Certainly we may have perspectives
that differ dramatically from those of our colleagues, and precisely "how"
to engage in dialogue without allowing it to degenerate into argument
and destructive forms of interaction is a continuing challenge. But as
Miller suggests above, disagreements—even vehement ones—can be
open, honest, and valued as evidence of a healthy community of dissensus. Indeed, racism, sexism, and homophobia—and their correspon-
ding actions—are among the attitudes that demand forthright response
and concerted redress. Acts of violence and abuse in the classroom,
among colleagues, and beyond the walls of the ivory tower need immediate and effective action. But most bitter academic disagreements are far
removed from the seriousness of these issues. Even those that are tied in
complex ways with objectionable attitudes—such as disagreements over
narrow and traditional definitions of the canon and of pedagogy—do not
demand the swift, harsh response that untempered anger motivates.
Processes of change over highly political and socially charged issues such
as those just mentioned can be long and difficult. The energy of anger can
be better directed toward a sense of long-term commitment to problem
solving rather than counter-productive attacks and immediate, harsh, and
personal responses.

Regretably, academic tempers flare often over far, far less important disagreements. Those of us who have been in this profession for several years may have seen individuals practically go to war over such minor issues as seating arrangements at department meetings and the necessary redirection of staff time away from coffee making. We must self-define in ways that allow us to process challenges to our opinions as something other than affronts to our self-worth and sense of professional and personal primacy. If we self-reflect and self-textualize as suggested above— accept our own fallibility and that we are part of a community that demands our collegial activity and investment—then we should be able to disagree openly and even vigorously without engaging in hurtful and personal attacks. If others are going to process our disagreement as an attack—even if it is gently and self-reflexively presented—we can do little to control their problematic attitudes and processings. Certainly we can better strategize for the future once we do know about such reactions, and self-protect and/or act with compassion as the situation warrants. However, if collegiality and community remain explicit and oft-articulated goals of the department, then at the very least individuals will be encouraged by example and group norm to self-reflect and de-personalize before responding in inflammatory and counterproductive fashion.

5. Finally, our local "success" derives from our understanding of local history and the genesis of local behaviors.

The texts of our institutions are complex ones, and systems of behavior and power not only have synchronic aspects but diachronic ones as well. Talk with senior colleagues, staff, and administrators about the histories of departmental and institutional norms. Current behaviors and tensions may seem bizarre and unaccountable until we learn about struggles over priorities and forms of institutional self-definition that may date back years or even decades. To understand how current norms and behaviors developed is to understand how they may be altered and also just how invested certain individuals may be in protecting them, even if they are stunningly anachronistic. Indeed, we might take our knowledge of the "new historicist" analysis of texts and apply it to the text of our own local environments. While our university's catalog will no doubt offer a timeline of its history, that is only one of the many "histories" that will emerge upon more careful scrutiny. As we talk to colleagues, support staff, and administrators, we should remember that their versions of events and accounting for current norms and behaviors are also always tendentious and incomplete (as ours would be), even as we recognize the powerful effect those memories and belief systems will have on how others judge us and our work, and also how successful we may be in any attempt to bring about change.

We are texts to each other and, finally, as readers of those texts we must be willing and able to recognize textual patterns. Thus if a colleague proves himself or herself to be consistently unreliable, I (as a competent reader) shouldn't expect that pattern to change miraculously. While I am not saying that such unreliable behavior is ever laudable, I am suggesting that if I place trust in individuals who have proven themselves untrustworthy, I must accept responsibility for my decision to do so. There is an entirely different book that could be written on the topic of how best to respond to psychologically unstable, actively destructive, or simply passive and lazy colleagues. I do not wish to linger on those extremes here. We should learn from the past, learn whom we can trust and upon whom we can depend, and value those individuals very highly. And to those responsible and reliable individuals especially, we should often express our gratitude.

~

"Ownership" as I have been using the term throughout this study means a willingness to take responsibility for our reactions, attitudes, and behaviors. While we will often find ourselves in less than ideal circumstances, our responses to those circumstances—often far more than the circumstances themselves—will determine our degree of contentment and the future course of our departments and universities. One of the biggest challenges facing young academics is deciding how and to what extent to "identify" with their current academic affiliation. I want to take a couple of concrete, if somewhat stark, examples here, fictionalized somewhat from the departmental experiences of a colleague at a neighboring institution.

Professor A arrives in his new department with what one might call a chip on his shoulder. He considers the job he has taken far "beneath" him because of the teaching load and lack of opportunity to instruct doctoral students (the department only offers an M.A.). He complains about the lack of funding for his research, treats his colleagues with barely concealed disdain, keeps the door to his office shut even during posted office hours, calls in sick often, and argues with staff members over perceived slights to his "authority." As unaware as he is, he is then very surprised when he receives unfavorable personnel reviews (he publishes, but that is all he does) and finally manages to find a job at another university, leaving town after handing the department chair a brusque resignation letter during the last week of the semester. The students with whom he had contact are demoralized, overall department morale has suffered because of his irritability, and the program within the department with which he was affiliated has suffered from his inattention.

Professor B also has career plans and ambitions. She also desires to teach doctoral students one day and is similarly concerned about the lack of local funding for research, but also takes her commitment to her present position seriously. While she does send out an occasional letter of application when an attractive position opens up at another institution, she has also mentally affiliated herself with her current institution for the long term. This means that certain aspects of that institution—the outdated design of the English major and the meager funding for conference travel—are ones that she devotes herself to altering in methodical ways. Although she does receive and take another position five years after arriving on campus, she leaves it a far better place than she found it and has earned the respect and gratitude of her colleagues and students. If that other offer had not come through, she had already started to make her present environment one in which she could thrive.

Both individuals had the same jobs and similar goals but had very different attitudes. The contrast between them may seem exaggerated but, in fact, it is not. I have seen firsthand what has happened to the Professor A's who never received another offer; they become bitter individuals who are wholly undependable—or worse, actively malevolent—colleagues. And I have seen the payoffs for the Professor B's who never received another offer; they are respected and rewarded locally for their earnest efforts, and they are, in fact, *happy*. Academic free agency, when it is exercised at the expense of colleagues and one's own equanimity, is a highly destructive force. One's loyalty to a particular institution is certainly not the issue here. Rather, it is one's attitude about the communal responsibilities that go along with any job, and the personal payoffs garnered while working to make a program or department a better place for the colleagues and students that one may leave behind after an early- or mid-career move, or perhaps retirement.

∽

Thus I wish to emphasize strongly that future possibilities and potentials—and many of them locally defined—should continue to invigorate us. This is as true for senior colleagues as it is for new hires. I believe that one of the unhealthiest attitudes plaguing institutions and, often, individual lives is nostalgia. In focusing on the (usually misremembered) past we invariably ignore the richness of the present and the energizing possibilities for the future. Moreover, nostalgia often becomes an easy justification for avoiding hard work; it is akin to cynicism in the inertia it fosters. Even when the past being evoked *is* accurately remembered as happy and productive, lingering on that past still wastes time. But, more often, in evoking a "golden era" from the past, the challenges and complexities of the present are magnified and overdramatized. The fuzzy lens that renders that past "golden" usually renders the present equally blurry and often threatening.

Thus one of the greatest challenges facing concerned faculty—and certainly administrators—is ensuring that the energy and attention of a department—both its senior and junior members—remain focused on the present and especially on the future. As I mentioned in a previous chapter, strategic planning is often scorned these days as a simple-minded waste of time. I certainly agree that far too often universities and other large institutional bodies oversell strategic planning and waste their personnel's time in participating in complex processes that can result in clichéd mission statements that often sound like ad copy. But even the most jaded and skeptical faculty can benefit enormously from the opportunity to talk in sustained fashion about their collective existence today and tomorrow. The same sort of energy that individuals can derive from active career planning can also benefit a department or other group that sets out goals and formulates plans to achieve them. If a group's energies are focused on ways to improve interpersonal communication, on articulating current strengths upon which to build, and on a few concrete goals to strive for by the end of an academic year, a planning discussion can assuage fears and relieve the tensions that come from isolation and from existing in dissensus. Most importantly, it can replace nostalgia with the more positive force of understanding the present and embracing the future. Cynicism, too, can hardly withstand the force of articulating and achieving precise and reasonable goals in the near future. But that achievement is key, of course, otherwise cynicism becomes validated and entrenched.

Some of the most compelling responses that I have received to pre-sentations of the material contained in this book have centered on the need to emphasize institutional constraints on any exercise of agency. Certainly, and as I have made clear throughout this book, those con-straints and all such synchronic limitations are real and must be recog-nized. But what is true today is not necessarily true tomorrow. One or two energetic department members can make a tremendous difference, for energy and collegiality can be infectious, just as inertia and cynicism can be. In organizing and spearheading the achievement of modest collective goals, a concerned coalition of hard-working and forward-thinking facul-ty can help reinvigorate an entire department, as well as effect important changes in policy, curriculum, or support for teaching or research. Indeed, personal investment, thoughtful challenge, and positive steps toward change are my responsibility and yours. We can work thoughtfully over weeks, months, and years, as individuals, as groups of community mem-bers, and as administrators, to effect change. Thus in the following talk-ing points, I want to offer a few concrete suggestions for thinking about the future, about change, and about investing ourselves thereby in our departments and institutions. In seeing our future as itself a text that we are involved every day in writing and revising, in discussing and analyz-ing, we can discover in our relationships with our communities an intel-lectual depth as well as the potential for both creativity and the exercise of our very best analytical skills.

Textualizing Institutional Change

1. Assess the possibilities for effecting change.

If we have fully invested ourselves and our professional identities in the present and future of our departments and universities, we may find aspects of it that desperately need attention. The design of the major or graduate program may not have changed in a decade or more. Commit-tee structures may be inefficient or anachronistic given evolving depart-ment needs. The communal intellectual life of the institution may be languishing. Of course here, as with processes of individual goal setting, specificity is key. What is it *precisely* that we would like to see change in our department or our university and how willing *are we* to take the primary responsibility for effecting those changes?

By engaging in both sychronic and diachronic analysis of the text of our institution and its norms and behaviors, we can begin the process of deciding how much time and energy we may wish to devote to working on curriculum, on program redesign or policy, or even on morale. But certainly we cannot do so effectively and in a self-protective manner if we have not done our homework. Read the institutional text slowly, carefully, and thoroughly; take notes, consult authority, and work methodically toward a broad understanding, before beginning a process of revisionary interpretation and argumentation. Discover which changes are possible and which may be impossible. For example, you may be able to change the distribution of departmental resources to offer greater support for faculty research, but you may never be able to change the institution's or system's fixed teaching load. Some institutional norms you may simply have to live with.

2. Prioritize changes.

Just as with scheduling any other professional work, we must set out clear goals and priorities. Even the most energetic of us cannot work effectively on our teaching, on our research, and, at the same time, on the complete overhaul of our department, its curriculum, and our institution's hiring policies. We have very real limits, of time and energy and patience, and also perhaps of stores of goodwill upon which we can draw as we negotiate with others whose priorities or beliefs may be very different from our own.

As we prioritize our changes, it is always useful to build our emerging plans into written schedules. We always do so with classes when we pass out syllabi and delineate how the work of the semester will proceed. We should do so as well with our writing projects as we plan the research, drafting, and revision stages of an essay or book. I am suggesting now that we also always do the same prioritization and careful planning with our work vis-à-vis the texts of our institutions. Of course we may discover later that our priorities must shift given the reality of our situation and the resistance to change that we encounter, but we must at least begin the process with our needs, desires, and specific goals articulated clearly. If we do not know what we want, why we want it, and what is most important to us, we are doomed from the outset.

3. Do a cost/benefit analysis for initiating and effecting specific changes.

It is very important that any untenured person thinking about taking on a project that involves departmental or institutional change consider carefully the risks he/she is running. Curricular change, departmental reorganization, shifts in priorities or institutional identity, even the creation of discussion or reading groups, may irritate entrenched faculty who are highly invested in the current system, however dysfunctional it may be. This is why a careful reading and thorough understanding of the history of current policies, behaviors, and norms is vital; we must be able to judge the intensity of any resistance to change that we will find among our colleagues and administrators, and where possible support for change may come.

Let me offer a concrete example. Let us say a couple of junior faculty members in an English department decide that it is time to change the major to incorporate a "theory" requirement for all students. In their opinion, the change is long overdue, and the need for it is clear. But unless they carefully research how and why their point of view may or may not be shared by other faculty in the department, they may be embroiling themselves in a controversy that will have serious career repercussions. Their first task must be to ask who believes what, why they believe it, and how intensely they hold their opinions. If those opinions are very intensely held, what are the specific consequences of a challenge to a policy reflecting those opinions, whether unsuccessful or (perhaps with an even greater likelihood of retaliation) successful? I have seen very worthwhile curricular changes, such as the one just described, fail in ways that generated terrible bitterness and divisiveness, and with the consequences of delayed tenure and promotion because individuals did not "read" their colleagues carefully or accurately. These were avoidable consequences if those individuals had used the same skills in interpreting their institutions as they used in interpreting the texts of eighteenth-century drama or the Victorian novel.

Indeed, trusted colleagues and administrators should be able to tell us about precise repercussions we should anticipate. Though it is hardly necessary to abandon all of our plans just because we discover we may irritate a few people, we should be realistic about our own need to protect our job and our time. If an attempt at a relatively small change is going to take months of negotiation, anger many of our senior colleagues, create long-term "enemies," and perhaps end in failure because of entrenched resistance, we need to consider carefully if such an endeavor is really worth the effort. Perhaps it is, but we should do our homework about the costs we may have to pay so we can truly decide if the benefits—which also may be considerable—outweigh them. Doing such analysis vis-à-vis our various possible projects will allow us to prioritize them wisely.

4. Understand exactly how change can occur at a given institution.

We should never embark on a process of change unless we know exactly how to make it happen. Which committees, if any, must approve our plans? Which administrators are responsible for passing judgement on them? What are the protocols for seeking consultation, and what forms of concurrence are required or expected? Something as relatively small as not knowing which forms to use and how to fill them out appropriately can undercut or lay waste our best plans. If we are taking on a controversial change, one that we know may meet resistance and anger colleagues, any sloppiness can become a weapon used effectively against us. And that sloppiness also becomes part of some people's perception of our professionalism and ability.

Again, textualizing our work can help us enormously. Many of us use outlines as we move through our writing projects; other professional projects warrant similar care. I often create a simple flowchart so I know all of the component parts of a change process and a timeline for the completion of its component parts. This clear, even graphic, delineation is especially helpful if we are part of a group process for change, where a precise division of responsibilities is key to success.

5. Understand the (possibly very long) timeline that change may require and commit to that timeline only after careful thought and planning.

One of the reasons that curriculum stays the same for decades, that no progress is made toward redefining departmental advising duties or research expectations, and that our larger professional norms themselves go wholly unaddressed, is simply that change can take many years to effect. Of course, we will not be working every day for that length of time on a given project—we may be waiting for months for a committee to examine and make a decision about a proposal—but we certainly must begin any such a process with an honest assessment of the time we must devote to a project and that will be needed to bring it to completion.

The consequences of *not* beginning with such an assessment are significant. If we take on a very difficult or controversial change project and simply fail to complete it, we may not only do ourselves great harm professionally—with colleagues and administrators who were also investing energy and hope in the project—but we also may make any subsequent efforts at bringing about the same or similar changes all the more difficult if not impossible. One of the points that I make throughout this book is that we *can* achieve many of our goals if we are honest, patient, and well organized. Processes of important, long-term change in which we prove ourselves to be muddled, impatient, and/or disorganized can wreck our careers and relationships with colleagues. As indicated earlier, that activity becomes part of the text of our professional self-identities that others will read and to which they will respond. And for those texts—of our own behaviors—we are ultimately responsible.

6. Reconsider your priorities and protect yourself if change becomes considerably more costly and dangerous than anticipated.

We may do all of our homework, know exactly how it is possible to bring about the changes that we wish to see occur, talk with colleagues and administrators to gauge their degree of support or resistance, and then embark enthusiastically on an important and seemingly achievable project. But we cannot anticipate all the difficulties that may arise or be assured that everyone is being wholly honest with us about their opinions concerning our efforts. Just because we are responsible and forthright does not mean that all of our colleagues and administrators will be.

Suddenly we may find that resistance to our plans emerges where we anticipated none. Colleagues may declare themselves unalterably opposed to the changes we are working on. Administrations may change, and we suddenly find little support from our new chair or dean. New rules may emerge or new roadblocks put up that make the timetable much longer and the workload much more burdensome than we could ever have imagined. Especially if you are untenured and you sense that you are risking your job in ways that you could not have foreseen, be self-protective and consider altering your plans and priorities. In our writing projects, we sometimes alter our theses as we discover new information, deepen our research, and encounter alternate opinions. We should use the same care in our reading of and argumentation concerning our institutional texts. Even if you are tenured and secure, if you sense that new obstacles mean that you are expending vast amounts of time and energy that you desperately need to allocate elsewhere, you may wish to reconsider your investment in the process.

The first rule is that we gather all of the knowledge we can, make a wise decision to commit to a process, and then see the process through to completion. Too often many of us simply abandon projects because they are harder or more tedious than we thought they would be. But if you suddenly discover that your job is "on the line" and you then decide to continue your efforts knowing very well that you may be terminated because of your activities, you *are* making a choice. Sometimes such courageous stances are fully warranted, but please make such decisions carefully.

∼

Yet as necessary as such a warning may be, I want to end this chapter on a much more positive note. I have seen departments improve dramatically because of individual faculty members and small groups of faculty deciding to shoulder the responsibility for challenging rancor and dysfunctionality, for building a healthy community of dissensus. The offering of praise and congratulations alone will go a long way toward building a more collegial environment or maintaining the health of already well-functioning community. But other, seemingly small actions and group activities can also foster collegiality. Discussion groups, brownbag lunch presentations of new research and pedagogical strategies, and even simple social activities can help build a sense of shared purpose and productive communication across the lines of dissensus. Administrators—chairs in particular—have a tremendous responsibility for fostering an environment of collegial support and dialogue. But no faculty member should make the mistake of saying "the chair should do something about morale!" Any one person can make an enormous difference in initiating the activities above, and no one has more responsibility for doing so than you or I. Of course the success of morale-building work, in particular, depends upon its shared quality; if I initiate such activities, then my first responsibility must be to welcome your participation. Of course, not all faculty will respond positively to such an invitation. I have to remind myself, even as I express to you, that we should never be discouraged because a few rancorous individuals react cynically or destructively. All we can do is express and act upon our desire for collegial exchange.

This book is my best attempt to welcome all members of this profession into sharing the work of creating a new sense of collegial respect and support, of building and maintaining morale and community. We may disagree profoundly, and in an administrative capacity or committee vote I may make a decision that does not meet your desires, and vice versa, but finally, we depend upon each other for the well-being of our professional lives.

Textualizing Success

*W*hat does "success" mean? Is it the completion of a single, spectacular project or is it a quality of day-to-day existence? Is it a particular award or proof of professional recognition or an attitude, an inner state of equanimity? These are questions that each of us needs to ponder carefully in thinking through our concrete professional goals and priorities and how those intersect with our personal lives. My point throughout this book is not that we can ever define "success" finally or wholly on our own terms, spurning or ignoring larger professional belief systems, but that we *can* critically engage those larger values and adapt them—even dispense with some of them—as we take responsibility for our career choices, attitudes, and behaviors. Stressful situations, accidents, and unhappy outcomes are inevitable in every life. No amount of planning and scheduling can eliminate them. However, academic careers often involve considerable material and job security, fairly agreeable working conditions, and a remarkable freedom to choose projects and day-to-day priorities. None of my friends employed outside of the academy has a professional life that compares qualitatively to my own. They are stunned (as am I) when they hear academics complain loudly and frequently about their jobs. Yes, some specific academic employment situations are problematic, oppressive, or even abusive, but most of us employed in tenured or tenure-track positions are very, very lucky to have the jobs we have.

Recognizing that no career or personal life will be without its stresses, crises, and contretemps, our continuing challenge is how to weather those and sustain a sense of—dare I say it?—happiness and fulfillment. Such equilibrium cannot come from monomaniacal workaholism, but neither can it come from passivity. Rather, as emphasized throughout this book, it must derive from a supple awareness of both the text of ourselves and the context(s) in which we work and live, a continuing exploration of our own agency and a willingness to accept what we cannot change, a sense of self-reliance alongside contributions to and a recognition of our continuing reliance upon others. Success is never a static state; for me, it is a movement and an ongoing project, one pursued with intensity, flexibility, and self-awareness. This brief conclusion challenges you to textualize success for yourself. Here—as a postscript—is another small piece of my "script." I hope to be allowed to read yours someday.

Intensity is a quality that I have explored implicitly throughout this book, but by which, as I hope is clear now, I do not mean careerism or perfectionism. Here, intensity refers to an attitude of eagerness and a desire to grapple openly and energetically with the most difficult problems and intellectual quandaries encountered in my professional and personal lives. Indeed, living "intensely" entails for me a devotion to breaking down some of the boundaries between those lives, certainly between what I *read* and what I *do*. It is to commit myself to finding ways of putting abstract, intellectual theory into practice, a clichéd goal perhaps, but one horribly underrealized in our profession.

In fact, making that connection between the context of my reading and the text of my own life has long been a personal passion. I'm not sure when I first came across Walter Pater's 1868 conclusion to *The Renaissance*, probably in my mid-teens, by way of my interest in Oscar Wilde. But I do know that by the time I reached college in the late 1970s, Pater's injunction to "burn always with [a] hard, gem-like flame," his equation of maintaining such "ecstasy" with "success in life" (189), had left an indelible mark upon me. To understand fully the impact of these words, I suppose it is also necessary to place my reading of Pater in the context of my adolescent struggles with existentialism—specifically my encounters with Sartre and Nietzsche—and the crisis that we all face in this late modern world in confronting the question of how to *make* meaning in life, how to find happiness and fulfillment in an existence lacking intrinsic truth or purpose.

It would be easy to dismiss this as a predictably, uniquely adolescent struggle, but to do so would be to avoid conveniently—nervously, even—some of the base-level questions and anxieties that inevitably haunt all lives, personal and professional. It would be to avoid asking the hard question: "why even bother?" Why devote oneself to anything? Why bother committing to any process or project? Why forego the immediate pleasures of procrastination or self-pity for different and only possible satisfactions later on? Really, why even bother getting out of bed in the morning?

Speaking in a way that resonates with some of Sartre's exhortations (particularly in "Existentialism is a Humanism"), Pater still helps me answer that question:

> [W]e are all under sentence of death but with a sort of indefinite reprieve. . . : we have an interval, and then our place knows us no more. Some spend that interval in listlessness, some in high passions, the wisest, at least among "the children of this world," in art and song. For our one chance lies in expanding this interval, in getting as many pulsations as possible into the given time. Great passions may give us this quickened sense of life, ecstasy and sorrow of love, the various forms of enthusiastic activity, disinterested and otherwise, which come naturally to many of us. Only be sure it is passion—that it does yield you this fruit of a quickened, multiplied consciousness. (190)

That, frankly, has long been a guiding pedagogical principle and a central purpose throughout this book: to work to quicken and multiply the consciousness of my students and my readership; to urge you, in this case, to get as many pulsations as possible into your given time; to show how I have found a passionate and (in both a Paterian and more personal sense) "successful" career in the academy; and to encourage your own work in reading the texts of your careers and goals, thereby quickening and multiplying a larger professional dialogue and sense of self-awareness. The question that will always linger—whether or not we wish to admit it or confront it—is why bother? This book as a whole has worked to provide an extended answer. The best brief reiteration that I can offer here is that because *both* the processes and products of our "bothering" can lead to moments of "ecstasy" supported by an overall, sustainable sense of equanimity. And that, my friends, is "success" for me. While Pater may write, "Not the fruit of experience, but experience itself, is the end" (188), it is actually *both* that get me out of bed in the morning and that comprise a "variegated, dramatic life" (188), as Pater terms it.

If such an argument appears tautological, perhaps it is. Indeed, perhaps *all* we have as meaning-making mechanisms *are* tautologies; what is important and real to us is that to which we decide to ascribe importance and meaning. And for those of us already—for whatever reason—fascinated by texts, who already self-define as critics, intellectuals, and analytical thinkers, we *can decide* to turn that energy and interest to a passionate interpretive project vis-à-vis our own professional lives. And in this and other activities we *can decide* that our tautologies will be life- and community-affirming ones. Our writing, our teaching, and our professional community building provide many and always-changing opportunities for creating a network of meaning: by building bridges between our theories and practices; by integrating our broadest political/social goals and our day-to-day institutional activities; and by linking our intellectual principles with our concrete actions toward colleagues, students, and administrators. Indeed, this is a quickened, multiplied consciousness that encompasses both my professional and personal lives. It is, in short, my passion.

But to endure, that passion must retain a certain mobility and flexibility, as well as intensity. To burn intensely does not necessarily mean burning out if new and changing sources of fuel are tapped (to push the metaphor perhaps too far). But allowing such change in our own lives to occur necessarily means giving up our claim to static, definitive authority, to having already found that "key to all mythologies." Of course, neither sloppiness nor inconsistency is ever justifiable in a profession that has legitimate standards of judgement and in which people depend upon each other as colleagues and in pedagogical relationships. Flexibility and responsibility can go hand in hand. Indeed, my degree of flexibility is both my choice and my responsibility. Recognizing its communal implications is a key component of "ownership" as this book defines that term.

That is what I have meant throughout this discussion by self-awareness and the responsibilities that attend self-reflexivity, not self-obsession or paralyzing self-consciousness. An ownership of our communal existence can disrupt our tendencies toward solipsism and intellectual isolationism, even as we are focused on self-articulated goals and plans for achieving them. An awareness of our communal lives will only be paralyzing if we demand perfection of ourselves and are therefore terrified of the imperfection-locating judgements of others. If, however, we accept our own fallibility and the always imperfect contributions that we will make to a flow of conversation that inevitably continues through and past us, then self-awareness only carries with it the necessary burden of being accountable to ourselves and others for our articulations, decisions, priorities, and action plans. Certainly it is to retain that multiplied consciousness that presses us to consider the implications of our behavior, not only for ourselves but also for our colleagues, students, friends, and family. It is to open ourselves up to the learning opportunities that a vigorous communal existence always provides. It is, to appropriate one of George Eliot's most vivid and provocative metaphors, to retain an awareness of the web that connects us to our departments, to our colleagues across the nation, and to the many strands of national/international political and social life.

Our professional lives provide us with extraordinary opportunities and challenges in that regard. Critic Alan Mintz points out that Eliot captures vividly a modern world

> in which man's new means of realizing himself will be in his own works. If in the past a man could realize himself by occupying a position in society that required him to do nothing in particular—a gentleman being a man who could afford not to work—the modern era will see men judged by the works, beyond land and children, they leave behind them. No longer merely a compromising struggle for livelihood, work has been transformed into an impassioned struggle to change the world.
>
> Since value is so firmly rooted in significant work, the special anxieties of [her] novel's characters are for the success of their vocational projects: fears of incompletion, insignificance, interference, and incapacity. (57)

Certainly those anxieties today can drive us to an unceasing, relentless drive for production, for narrow, individualistic achievement at the expense of others, for tangible and continuous proof that we are valuable. But if we lift this "reading" of vocation and vocational anxieties *out of* the safe, circumscribed (and, yes, sexist language-riddled) world of literary analysis and if we *textualize* ourselves through this reading, can something more supple and sustainable result from the combination? I believe it can.

Certainly I would never deny the desirability of finding a sense of vocation and seeking fulfillment through it. Dorothea Brooke's own long unsatisfied vocational desires not only hang over the novel *Middlemarch*, and the world that it explores but also our own professional and personal lives: "For a long while she had been oppressed by the indefiniteness which hung in her mind like a thick summer haze over all her desire to make her life greatly effective. What could she do, what ought she to do?" (29–30). We are all faced with this same absolute, existential necessity of making meaning in our lives. And we in the academy have singular and stunning opportunities for engaging in an "impassioned struggle to change the world" in positive and effective ways. Let us not make Dorothea's mistake and tie ourselves to the dead hand of the past, to the Casaubonic or the Carlylean; even so, we should certainly learn from that past. Indeed, let us never be afraid of reading Eliot, Pater, Wayne Booth, Bill Reading, and others, and asking time and again "where am I in this text?"

This takes hard work in *actively choosing* to read differently, to act differently, and always with that quickened, multiplied consciousness. And this emphasis on active choice is the most useful aspect of another book well worth reading: Phillip McGraw's *Life Strategies: Doing What Works, Doing What Matters*. As with those of other pop psychologists, there is plenty in McGraw's book to irritate us: totalizing statements, sweeping generalizations, and a masculinist rhetoric that grates on one's nerves. But just as with more canonical writers—such as Pater and Eliot—such inevitable imperfections should never deter us from drawing from McGraw concepts that are helpful. In one of his most usefully provocative passages, McGraw urges us all to *accept responsibility*. He states this as his "Life Law #2":

> Acknowledge and accept accountability for your life. Understand your role in creating the results that are your life. Learn how to choose better so you have better.
>
> The law is simple: you are accountable for your life. Good or bad, successful or unsuccessful, happy or sad, fair or unfair, you own your life. . . .
>
> If you don't like your job, you are accountable. If your relationships are on the rocks, you are accountable. If you are overweight, you are accountable. If you don't trust members of the opposite sex, you are accountable.

If you are not happy, you are accountable. Whatever your life circumstance is, accepting this law means that you can no longer dodge responsibility for how and why your life is the way it is. (56–57)

While McGraw later goes on to qualify his assertions by saying that he is not blaming victims for the circumstances of their victimization, he does place responsibility for how to respond even to victimization squarely on the shoulders of the affected individual if that individual wants to recover a healthy and happy life.

Of course, one can qualify McGraw's assertions to the point of dismissing them and find all sorts of exceptions to this or other "Life Laws" he proposes. We intellectuals are very talented at thinking our way out of accepting responsibility by lingering in such exceptions and qualifications, but I'm not going to do that here. Instead, I want to urge—to plead, even—that we who are students of abstract, intellectually challenging theory need desperately to listen to such metatheoretical reminders that our own lives and careers always need critically examining as much as, perhaps much more than, the printed texts that we read and teach. No committee, no mentor, no institution, no organization (as powerful as the MLA may seem) is going to make our lives better. We may individually or collectively work to improve our lives and those of our students and colleagues, but finally we have to make that choice and take the initiative.

That assuming of responsibility has implications both for one's internal and external states of being, for one's relationships with students, colleagues, and administrators, for one's individual aspirations and plans for collective action. Furthermore, it challenges us as "critics" of texts and analysts of others' actions to move beyond simple criticism of our colleagues' inevitably flawed articulations into articulating our own ideals and best ideas. Granted, this means that we have to accept responsibility for those and accept the inevitable critique of colleagues—some of whom may not be willing to do anything other than simply find flaws in our work while not offering to replace it with anything—but so be it. If we are committed to change—in our personal lives, careers, institutions, and profession—no one is more responsible for initiating that change than we are.

Revolutionary acts and monumental campaigns are hardly necessary. To define change in such grandiose terms usually renders it impossible to imagine, commit to, or effect. This book will succeed if it prods a few readers into thinking about how to thank their colleagues more consistently, about how to present to doctoral students a wider variety of career paths as ones that are laudable and potentially very fulfilling, about how to forgive ourselves and others for mistakes, and about how to use our critical and analytical talents to work toward a measure of happiness in our professional and personal lives as well as the lives of those around us. None of us will succeed perfectly, but perfection is no worthy goal anyway. There is no key to all mythologies.

And with that Eliotian observation, I will leave you with a final connection to the very final passage of *Middlemarch*, Eliot's professional studies "text" to which we should all attend with care. Our finely touched spirits can still have their fine issues, though they may not be widely visible. Our full natures, like that river of which Cyrus broke the strength, may spend themselves in channels that have no great name on the earth. But the effects of our being on those around us *can* be incalculably diffusive, for the growing good of the world is partly (I would even say largely) dependent on unhistoric acts, and that things are not so ill with you and me as they might have been is half owing to the number who lived faithfully a hidden life and rest in unvisited tombs. As with Dorothea Brooke, none of us has an inward being so strong that it is not greatly determined by what lies outside of it.

But our medium is one in which ardent deeds may be undertaken. Ours is a conventual life desperately in need of reform.

Let us read carefully.

Appendix

Sample Professional Statement
Donald E. Hall

Linking my diverse set of publications and teaching interests is a consistent professional interest: "subjectivity," in its various manifestations. Influenced by and drawing upon the theories of Michel Foucault, Anthony Giddens, Judith Butler, Michel de Certeau, and others, my work to date has probed the bases by which standpoint epistemologies are established and, even more importantly, altered, through individualized acts of agency, through contact with an evolving social context, and through dialogue, directly interpersonal and more broadly intellectual. For the purposes of this work, discrete theories—queer, feminist, materialist, poststructuralist—are useful tools, but only partial truths.

After completing my current project—an investigation of academic identity—I will turn to an already contracted graduate-level introduction to "queer theory," which will include sustained investigations and textual applications of bisexual theory, as well as theories of race, class, and gender. Future projects include a study—tentatively entitled "The Ties That Bind: Victorian Classifications and Postmodern Perversions"—that integrates new and previously published work, and that examines the resonance of Victorian classification systems in contemporary pop cultural and radical sexual experimentations with "perversity." This work continues my career-long interest in the responsiveness of individual identity to concerted acts of challenge.

This emphasis on the potentials and limitations of personal agency also links my research with my pedagogy and service commitments. I run classes as workshops, in which students are given the bases for skillful acts of textual and intellectual intervention, but then must work dialogically within the classroom (where I play a key role, of course) to articulate, critically evaluate, and hone their applications. Similarly, I act within institutions to try to identify areas of stagnation that can respond to individual and collective efforts at rethinking and reinvigoration. The goal-setting skills that I bring to those processes, and the fulfillment that I derive from them, have led me recently to work in administration, where I am finding new opportunities for integrating "theory" and "practice." And outside the walls of the university, my ongoing commitment to social activism and community service is similarly motivated.

Thus as a teacher, scholar, administrator, colleague, and community member my work is imbued with an enthusiasm, and even an optimism, that comes from seeing all aspects of my professional life as interconnected and dependent for its very existence upon intellectual development through dialogue with others, through critical attachment to the most vexed questions of power, authority, and agency, and through a sense of creative potential in a professional life. While often turning to the past—Victorian and more recent eras—for textual representations of lives lived passionately, responsibly, and honestly (or otherwise), those turns are always motivated by a sense of urgency for evaluating the present and working toward a future that finds new ways of valuing difference and fulfilling the potential of intellectual concepts too often and unnecessarily divorced from the challenges and opportunities of everyday life.

References

Beck, Ulrich, Anthony Giddens, and Scott Lasch. *Reflexive Modernization: Politics, Tradition, and Aesthetics in the Modern Social Order.* Stanford, Calif.: Stanford University Press, 1994.

Bérubé, Michael. *The Employment of English: Theory, Jobs, and the Future of Literary Studies.* New York: New York University Press, 1998.

Bolker, Joan. *Writing Your Dissertation in Fifteen Minutes a Day.* New York: Holt, 1998.

Booth, Wayne C. *Critical Understanding: The Powers and Limits of Pluralism.* Chicago: University of Chicago Press, 1979.

Botshon, Lisa, and Siobhan Senier. "The 'How-to' and Its Hazards in a Moment of Institutional Change." In *Profession 2000,* 164–72. New York: Modern Language Association, 2000.

Burns, David D. *Feeling Good: The New Mood Therapy.* New York: Avon, 1992.

Carlson, Richard. *Don't Sweat the Small Stuff . . . and it's all small stuff.* New York: Hyperion, 1997.

———. *Don't Sweat the Small Stuff at Work.* New York: Hyperion, 1998.

Carlyle, Thomas. "Characteristics." In *A Carlyle Reader,* edited by G. B. Tennyson, 67–103. Cambridge: Cambridge University Press, 1984.

Davidson, Cathy N. "Them versus Us (and Which One of 'Them' is Me?)" In *Profession 2000,* 97–108. New York: Modern Language Association, 2000.

Davidson, Jeff. *The Complete Idiot's Guide to Managing Your Time.* 2d ed. New York: Alpha Books, 1999.

Eliot, George. *Middlemarch.* New York: Signet, 1981 [1872].

Falzon, Christopher. *Foucault and Social Dialogue: Beyond Fragmentation*. New York: Routledge, 1998.

Fish, Stanley. *Doing What Comes Naturally: Change, Rhetoric, and the Practice of Theory in Literary and Legal Studies*. Durham, N.C.: Duke University Press, 1989.

Giddens, Anthony. *The Consequences of Modernity*. Stanford, Calif.: Stanford University Press, 1990.

———. *Modernity and Self-Identity: Self and Society in the Late Modern Age*. Stanford, Calif.: Stanford University Press, 1991.

Gini, Al. *My Job, My Self: Work and the Creation of the Modern Individual*. New York: Routledge, 2000.

Goldsmith, John A., et al. *The Chicago Guide to Your Academic Career: A Portable Mentor for Scholars from Graduate School through Tenure*. Chicago: University of Chicago Press, 2001.

Hall, Donald E. "Professional Life (and Death) Under a Four-Four Teaching Load." In *Profession 1999*, 193–203. New York: Modern Language Association, 1999.

———, ed. *Professions: Conversations on the Future of Literary and Cultural Studies*. Urbana: University of Illinois Press, 2001.

———. "Response to Lisa Botshon and Siobhan Senier." In *Profession 2000*, 172–75. New York: Modern Language Association, 2000.

Heiberger, Mary Morris and Julia Miller Vick. *The Academic Job Search Handbook*. 3d ed. Philadelphia: University of Pennsylvania Press, 2001.

Lindenberger, Herbert. "Must We Always Be in Crisis?" *ADFL Bulletin* 29, no. 2 (1995): 5–9.

Lonchar-Fite, Patricia. "'We're not in Kansas Anymore': One Response to Hall's Discussion of the 4-4 Course Load." One English Department's Response to D. Hall Roundtable. SCMLA Convention. Sheraton Gunter Hotel, San Antonio. 11 November 2000.

McGraw, Philip. *Life Strategies: Doing What Works, Doing What Matters*. New York: Hyperion, 1999.

McKay, Matthew, Peter Rogers, and Judith McKay. *When Anger Hurts: Quieting the Storm Within*. Oakland, Calif.: New Harbinger Publications, 1989.

Miller, J. Hillis. "Vital Diversity: An Interview with J. Hillis Miller." In *Professions*, ed. Donald E. Hall. 224–35.

Mintz, Alan. *George Eliot and the Novel of Vocation*. Cambridge, Mass.: Harvard University Press, 1978.

Modern Language Association Committee on Professional Employment. *Final Report*. New York: Modern Language Association, 1997.

Moskowitz, Eva S. *In Therapy We Trust: America's Obsession with Self-Fulfillment*. Baltimore, Md.: Johns Hopkins University Press, 2001.

Nelson, Cary. *Manifesto of a Tenured Radical*. New York: New York University Press, 1997.

Pater, Walter. *The Renaissance: Studies in Art and Poetry*. Berkeley: University of California Press, 1980.

Perez, Hector. "SCMLA: Panel Introduction." One English Department's Response to D. Hall Roundtable. SCMLA Convention. Sheraton Gunter Hotel, San Antonio. 11 November 2000.

Quazi, Moumin. "A Post-Colonial Response to Donald Hall's 'Professional Life (and Death) Under a Four-Four Teaching Load.'" One English Department's Response to D. Hall Roundtable. SCMLA Convention. Sheraton Gunter Hotel, San Antonio. 11 November 2000.

Readings, Bill. *The University in Ruins*. Cambridge, Mass.: Harvard University Press, 1996.

Schubnell, Matthias. "Constructing 'A Joyous and Successful Career' With Your Family's Happiness in Mind: A Response to Donald Hall." One English Department's Response to D. Hall Roundtable. SCMLA Convention. Sheraton Gunter Hotel, San Antonio. 11 November 2000.

Showalter, English, et al. *The MLA Guide to the Job Search: A Handbook for Departments and Ph.D.s and Ph.D. Candidates in English and the Foreign Languages*. New York: Modern Language Association, 1996.

Tannen, Deborah. "Agonism in the Academy: Surviving Higher Learning's Argument Culture." *Chronicle of Higher Education* 31 March 2000: B7+.

———. *The Argument Culture: Stopping America's War of Words*. New York: Ballantine, 1998.

Toth, Emily. *Ms. Mentor's Impeccable Advice for Women in Academia*. Philadelphia: University of Pennsylvania Press, 1997.

Index